Jenny Kander

So will I comfort you...

Support for bereaved parents, their families, friends and counsellors

"As one whom his mother comforteth, so will I comfort you"

(ISAIAH 66:13)

Lux Verbi

Copyright © 1990 Lux Verbi
P O Box 1822, Cape Town
All rights reserved
Cover illustration by Tamar Kander
Set in 10 on 12 pt Plantin
Printed and bound by
National Book Printers
Goodwood, Cape
First edition, first print 1990
Second print 1992

ISBN 0 86997 338 X

DEDICATION:
*To The Compassionate Friends, S.A.
In deep appreciation for all that you have
taught me and for the quality of caring which
you offer fellow bereaved parents, siblings,
grandparents and other members of the immediate family.*

ACKNOWLEDGEMENTS:
*I wish to express my gratitude to my husband,
Yacov, for his unending patience and his faith in
my ability to write; to Linda Abelheim for her
help, constant encouragement and her insistence that I have a message to deliver; to
Annelize van der Ryst for her interest, support
and valuable advice; to Pat Baxter for her
discernment and willing assistance; to Richard
Cohn and Ric Matthews for so generously taking
the time to read the manuscript; to my son
Nadav and to Nicole for their unflagging interest and support, and to Tim Trollip who
nagged me for more than two years to write this
book.
   I have used a painting by Tamar, my
daughter, for the cover. I thank her most warmly
for its spaciousness and beauty, and acknowledge
both her and Joe for their faith in my work.
   I do not think I would have managed without
the help and forbearance of Tony Mansfield and
Elizabeth Horner. I want to acknowledge their
always being available when I needed them.
   To all those others, too numerous to mention,
who have been of assistance and had faith in this
book, I offer my thanks as well.*

Foreword

I first met her five weeks after my son Joel died.

At that time, I didn't think there was anything or anyone who could help me. I hurt all over, in every single part of my life – deeply and intensely; pain brimmed over under the weight of the single most immense mind- and life-altering experience of my existence . . . I had outlived my child.

I wanted him back. Nothing else mattered.

So will I comfort you . . . is Jenny speaking to you as she spoke to me. With the skill to put it all in writing, she uses its pages to help you take charge of your life once more.

This book will acknowledge and validate you. It will urge and encourage you. Its instinctive and uncanny logic will make sense where nothing else does. The gentle wisdom will warm and comfort you; the stillness and quietness will draw you into that suspension of pain towards a place where you can catch your breath.

So will I comfort you . . . is the closest thing to meaningful support that I know of. In the outrageous irreversibility of your child's death, Jenny Kander makes a difference.

If you are a bereaved parent, this book will help you.

LINDA ABELHEIM
National President:
The Society of The Compassionate Friends of S.A.

Contents

Part II: Siblings' grief

Part III: About bereavement, grief and healing

Part IV: Rites

Introduction

A bereaved parent asked: "Why does it still hurt after all this time?" I am not sure that there is one answer to so poignant a question, but perhaps this book can provide a perspective that will shed some light on grief and offer comfort for the suffering.

This book has grown out of many talks given over the past six years to the Johannesburg branch of The Compassionate Friends. They have been rewritten and updated to include information gained from spending time in groups and individually with grieving parents. Many new sections have been included to extend the scope of the content. It is addressed mainly to bereaved parents. To add to the material written for the professional I have chosen to speak directly to you who grieve.

In a number of the articles I have encouraged parents to seek professional help. A book can only deal with generalities whilst each person's circumstances and grief are beyond the obvious common denominators. For this reason I suggest counselling when matters become complicated for the mourner.

This book is not one that is likely to be read from cover to cover, but rather piece-meal according to which sections seem most relevant to the reader. There is of necessity some repetition where central themes must be referred to in different contexts. I apologise for this.

I have used the term "grief-work" a number of times. I define this with three "e's": to *endure,* consciously *experience,* and *express* all feelings.

For ease of reading I have decided to use "he", "him" and "his" when referring to the living child (whatever the gender), and "s/he", "his/her", etc. when writing about the child who died. It seems so important to encompass both son and daughter in the text when referring to the one who is being mourned. Taking into account the high level of sensitivity of bereaved parents I do not want those whose daughters have died to feel overlooked.

For the sake of brevity I have used the term "minister" throughout to refer to rabbis, priests, and all spiritual leaders, as relevant to your specific denomination.

Part I, entitled *Grieving and healing,* is sub-divided into coping in general, in specific situations, relationships and loss, grief related to the cause of death, and rites.

Part II, *Siblings' grief,* addresses itself to the concerns and difficulties of the surviving children. Hopefully it will assist you and your family members to meet their needs.

Part III, *Bereavement, grief and healing,* is written for counsellors, caregivers and anyone interested in the dynamics of grief and in helping the bereaved. Parents may find these articles of interest as well – but primarily they are designed to teach and extend the skills of those who counsel.

A book list precedes the bibliography and is included as a guide to further reading. It contains books that I have found most helpful.

It is my heartfelt wish that *So will I comfort you* will bring consolation, much needed support, and perspective to all who so bravely grieve and carry on.

I
Grieving and healing

THE EXISTENCE OF LOVE

I had thought that your death
Was a waste and a destruction,
A pain of grief hardly to be endured.
I am only beginning to learn
That your life was a gift and a growing
And a loving left with me.
The desperation of death
Destroyed the existence of love,
But the fact of death
Cannot destroy what has been given.
I am learning to look at your life again
Instead of your death and your departing.
MARJORIE PIZER

REBIRTH

I am emerging from an ocean of grief,
From the sorrow of many deaths,
From the inevitability of tragedy,
From the losing of love,
From the terrible triumph of destruction.
I am seeing the living that is to be lived,
The laughter that is to be laughed,
The joy that is to be enjoyed,
The loving that is to be accomplished.
I am learning at last
The tremendous triumph of life.
MARJORIE PIZER

These poems are reprinted with kind permission of the author.

How to cope . . .

A In general

1. Taking care of yourselves

I often see a glazed look in bereaved parents' eyes when I broach the subject of their taking care of themselves. That is a clue to the despair they feel. When I ask, "Do you hurt so much that you are not concerned about your health at all?" the look fades: "Yes, that's how I feel – nothing matters anymore."

You do matter.

And because you do, I want to set out for you the practicalities of self-care, and nurturing one another. In time you will realise, as have other bereaved parents, that healing *is* worthwhile and that attention to your general well-being is part of it and helps you to cope.

Because the death of your child affects every facet of your being we will look not only at the physical, but also at the emotional, intellectual, spiritual and social aspects.

● *Physical aspects*

☐ *Nourishment:* Appetite lessens in grief, or increases to compensate for the sense of emptiness. In either case it is essential that you eat nourishing and not "junk" food. Your nervous system is being severely taxed because grief continues for quite a time. Therefore you require increased amounts of the B vitamins, additional green leafy salads (including sprouts) vegetables and fruit. Protein and wholegrains (such as brown rice, unrefined cereals, wholewheat bread) will help to raise your energy level.

It seems so much effort to attend to meals, but please understand that gains in terms of your increased ability to manage make the effort well worthwhile.

Both alcohol and sugar reduce appetite, so they are to be taken in small quantities, if at all. Do try to have balanced meals.

If you feel unable to eat your normal amount of food at mealtimes, eat smaller quantities more often. This will ensure that you do get the nourishment you need, and that you are not uncomfortably full. Difficulty in swallowing is a common problem during bereavement; a brief relaxation exercise before the meal helps and also aids digestion. (See: *Relaxation and pain meditation*, p. 23).

Blessing food and giving thanks for it replace negative feelings with acceptance.

You may feel that you do not care whether you eat or not. Consider your family members. Consider too your distress, were you to die and your loved ones not eat or care for themselves. Are you not one of your own loved ones? Do you not have a responsibility to yourself and others?

☐ *Rest:* Without sufficient *sleep* or rest you are less able to deal adequately with your daily lives – even under normal circumstances. Grief is exhausting, so extra care is necessary to ensure your well-being.

Relaxation is discussed on p. 23, but I do want to point out that even if you cannot sleep, just knowing that you are *resting* can help you to relax. Nevertheless, if for nights on end you are not getting more than a few hours sleep, consult your doctor. He can give some assistance for just a few nights to break the pattern and restore your energy. Homeopathic preparations are also very helpful, harmless and non-addictive.

☐ *Exercise:* This is very important in times of grief, though you need to be aware of your altered endurance and energy levels and not overdo it. Besides toning up and restoring regularity to your system it can bring about a sense of well-being. It is also an excellent way of reducing stress and affords you a healthy tiredness that assists you to sleep. Exercise can take the form of a daily walk if you are not inclined to anything more strenuous.

☐ *Drugs and alcohol:* Assistance or escape? I deal fairly fully with this issue in the section titled *Crutches* (p. 20) so just a few additional comments will suffice:

Taking drugs such as tranquillisers, sleeping pills or alcohol blunts awareness of pain and thus brings some relief on a *short-term basis*. But as the effect wears off you find you are no further on in dealing effectively with your loss. All you have done is to alleviate the symptoms and postpone the grief-work necessary to resolve it.

Long-term benefits are the valuable ones and are brought about by facing your pain gradually, at your own natural pace and in your own way – but dealing with it. Weigh up the value of any "crutch" you are taking in terms of its long-term value to you. For instance, anti-depressants can only help if you use both the energy they release and the consequent easing of immobilising grief to work through your loss. Just passively taking tablets is no solution and undermines your already lowered sense of competence.

☐ *Physical contact:* Being held can be so comforting . . . but sometimes you do not want to be touched. You and your spouse may find you have opposite needs quite a lot of the time. People grieve and express themselves in dissimilar ways. So it is helpful to make your needs known and listen to those of your partner. Be prepared to be patient with yourself and each other. The way you feel right now will change in time but meanwhile you may have to make some compromises.

Sexual contact can bring great comfort and solace and does release stress, but sometimes a parent cannot bear the thought of engaging in the act that brought the deceased child into the world. Perhaps you feel that to have any enjoyment now is wrong, inappropriate. Indeed, often both a sense of disloyalty and of guilt interfere with the resumption of a normal sex life. "How can I find pleasure and forget my child when s/he is dead?" Or: "What right do I/we have to satisfaction . . .?"

There may be anger, an accusation of non-caring levelled at your spouse, and this can cause great hurt. Life does go on; your child would doubtless not wish you to cease living and mourn forever.

What would s/he want for you? Your renewed well-being and sharing, surely.

● *Intellectual aspects*
The instinctual response to any threat (of which loss is one) is to fight or flee. There are other means of dealing with threats, and the ability to think allows you choice.

Feelings are governed by thought; this means that you do have some control over how you are feeling. Let me give an example: If you think you cannot cope and will never come through your grief, you will feel panic-stricken, despairing. But if you choose to think that although this is a nightmare somehow you will manage to hold yourself together, you will feel some capability, some strength. So in taking care

17

of yourself be careful of the direction your thoughts take (up towards trust, or down into hopelessness). If you can see nothing but pain and loss it is valuable to explore other ways of viewing life and afterlife, though this is not something you will be able to do whilst still in a state of shock. (A minister may be helpful to you.)

Here are some guidelines:

☐ Know that the darkness will pass. It is natural for it to do so. The day does not refuse to dawn because preceded by night. In fact, we can trust light to repeatedly dispel blackness in the cycles of time.

☐ Be willing to go on with your life: to hope, and (in time) to let go of pain and to heal.

☐ Believe in recovery, in your ability to use this experience in such a way that it bears fruit. There is no crisis that does not have within it the potential for meaningful growth, but you must consciously choose it.

☐ Have patience with the grief process; you will have memory lapses, difficulty concentrating . . . but restoration will come.

● **Emotional aspects**

Prior to your own bereavement you may have known about emotional reactions to loss, but until the death of your child you were probably unaware of the range and intensity of feelings that are experienced.

Some of the ways that mourners use in trying to deal with these are useful and some are not. I will begin with those that bring healing:

☐ *Expressing* feelings is vital – but you must do so appropriately. This means getting relief from them whilst doing no harm to yourself, others, to pets, or even to property. For your well-being the expression of emotion must not be carried to exhausting extremes of severity or duration.

It is essential for both fathers and mothers to cry if you are able to. Be willing to vent your grief, anger and other feelings – in private if you are more comfortable with that – but preferably with someone who can understand, really listen and allow you to let go. It is in community with others that healing seems to take place most effectively.

☐ *Exploring* your grief responses is challenging and valuable if it brings you greater insight into the mourning process, and increased

18

self-knowledge. Exploration is best entered into with someone who can assist you, such as a grief-counsellor. A bereaved parent, especially one who has at least to some extent come through his/her grief, can be an invaluable help. To the extent that you are able to endure (rather than block) your feelings, experience them and give them expression, you are doing the grief-work necessary to recovery.

☐ If you are able at times *to stand back* from your emotions, to detach yourself for a while and just observe them rather than becoming submerged, you will find it a relief and much less exhausting. For instance: when angry, recognise it but watch your anger objectively, knowing that it will pass and that you do not necessarily have to get involved. This may be a strange concept to you, but it is worth a try. You will begin to realise that you are not a victim of your grief but have some control over it. I am not suggesting an unrealistic splitting off from your experiences, but rather an involvement with them as observer.

☐ *Avoiding* or escaping from pain may take the form of sometimes blocking, denying the reality of the death. It seems so unreal, so impossible, unacceptable. For many months this is a natural and necessary response to the overwhelming sense of loss. When avoidance becomes an ongoing refusal to recognise the reality, it interferes with the healing process. Timing is individual and depends upon so many factors which relate to each circumstance and family that I cannot give you time-limits. If you feel that you are making no progress after a number of months it might be wise to talk to someone who understands the grief process and can give you some perspective.

● *Spiritual aspects*
The death of a loved person causes many people to question God, their religion, their faith and what life and death is all about. I have seen parents come closer to God through their loss and many who have moved away. Some are angry and reject Him, whilst some try to accept that it was His will . . .

Whatever your view, I encourage you to explore what you think and feel, your beliefs about life and death, the universe and your place in it. It can of course be of great value to speak to your minister if you are needing the perspective that he can give you. Surprisingly perhaps, the grief situation can often spur your growth, challenging you to look deeper, further . . . Your spiritual needs should not be ignored, and indeed they often clamour for attention in crisis situations.

Many bereaved parents reject Deity in despair and anger: either saying that there cannot be a God, or that one who allows the death of a child is not one to whom they can or wish to pray. It helps when I tell them that He is greater than human thoughts and emotions, and can understand. It is natural, in the face of such devastating pain, to feel great anger at God. There is no need for self-reproach. Under such duress your rejection and rage is actually a dynamic relationship with Him. In time the tone thereof will change and healing can take place, unless you choose to maintain your anger – at great cost. Behind the storm is God's unconditional loving acceptance and the resultant peace when you are ready for it.

If you think that you cannot pray, cannot find words, just state from your heart how it is for you, what you feel and what your difficulties are. Just talk, or shout if you need to, but share who you are and what you are going through. (See the section titled *Spiritual needs* on p. 53.)

● *Social aspects*
Grief is a dislocating experience. At times it seems as if you have lost your old familiar self and are out of touch with others too. And your needs change so rapidly: "I want to get out and be with people. I can't stand being alone" and then "I feel safe at home and I want to be by myself" . . . Perhaps you begin to wonder if you are losing your mind.

All of this is normal. Be patient with yourself. To the extent that you can communicate your feelings and needs to family members, colleagues and friends you will feel less pressure to act "normally". Recognise that others who are grieving are also having difficulty coping. For a large part of the first year of a bereavement (maybe even longer), it is likely to be almost impossible for you to assist other grieving family members to deal with their pain. You may not even notice their needs. It makes sense, therefore, to ask for help.

Once again I say: You do matter; take care of yourself. Set small goals in terms, guided by the above; just one step at a time and you will be making progress, day by day.

2. Crutches

The subject of crutches is interesting and not one about which we need necessarily be negative.

Consider this analogy: you have broken your leg; the doctor sets it to immobilize the bone while it heals. To facilitate getting about you use crutches. Under normal circumstances a walker, a pulley or a wheelchair is not needed. When the bone has healed the plaster is removed, the crutches discarded and with the aid of gentle exercise you return to normal. You do not continue to use your crutches or any other aid thereafter. You have not been ill, only disabled for a period.

Now when you are bereaved you are not ill but, for a time, disabled. And because grief is primarily emotional you have a far wider choice and greater flexibility in terms of coping than had you broken your leg.

In this context there are a few questions that must be asked:

● *What coping skills do you possess?*

To assess your own coping skills ask yourself how, before the death of your child, you dealt with stress (whether due to loss, pressure, or strain). Did you manage successfully, that is without being traumatized or incapacitated? Were you able to deal with the issue at hand in a way that resolved it whilst for the most part carrying on with your daily life? Or have you always used a crutch – an external aid? I am not suggesting that the loss of a child is comparable to most other traumas, but you can get a fair idea of your inner strength and resourcefulness by taking an honest look at your coping ability. There is a great variety of ways that people deal with stress: some keep busy, some withdraw, some talk it through, some cry . . .

Generally drugs or alcohol are not necessary to help deal with grief.

● *Which appropriate crutches are available to you?*

☐ You can rely on your own ability to deal with the situation of loss, and on the natural process of grief which, unless interfered with, is one of rehabilitation and healing.

☐ You can enter into a counselling relationship with someone who understands the dynamics of grief and has the skills to help you find your way through the confusing and difficult period of mourning.

☐ You can choose therapy if you find that the loss of your child brings out some unresolved problems that require in-depth work to resolve.

Both counselling and therapy are entered into for a limited period: they should never become lifelong addictions!

☐ You can use medication: certainly there are exceptions when drugs

21

are necessary to help people cope with grief – tranquillizers, anti-depressants and sleeping tablets – but generally you will be able to manage without them. Whether to use them or not is a decision you will have to make.

When tranquillizers and "something to make you sleep" are pressed upon you, a natural response is one of heightened anxiety and consequent acceptance of the proffered "help". It is not a reasoned response. I often feel tempted to suggest to those who unnecessarily encourage tablet-taking that they themselves take the dose and calm down! Many people who took tranquillizers to help them cope with the funeral had no recollection afterwards of the event, and felt they had missed an important rite.

Then there is the issue of addiction. Before agreeing to take any drugs ask your doctor to supply full information as to their effectiveness, side-effects and any other risk factors involved. Keep him informed as to how you are responding to the prescribed dose and do not take a repeat prescription to the chemist month after month without fresh medical advice.

Consistent sleeping problems, that is not getting more than three to five hours of sleep nightly for an extended period, might well cause you to feel unable to cope with your grief and your daily activities. It is wise to ask your doctor for help and to suggest that you take what he prescribes for two or three nights only. Usually this is sufficient to give the much-needed rest and to break the pattern (even if only temporarily) of grief-induced insomnia. Then you do not run the risk of physiological or psychological dependency.

Depression is a natural reaction to grief and can, under normal circumstances, be worked through without recourse to medication. The support of a counsellor or therapist can be most valuable, though it is often not essential. When depression becomes incapacitating and prolonged, medical advice must be sought, for anti-depressants may be appropriate.

Suicidal thoughts are normal during bereavement. If they are intense and/or frequent it is wise to have counselling or therapy, at least for a while.

Homeopathic remedies are effective, non-harmful, non-addictive and are made from natural substances. A skilled homeopath is an excellent help to the bereaved.

● *To what extent and for how long should you use these crutches?*

The extent and duration of support required depend on the following: your individual situation – whether personal strength is sufficient, family and/or friends are supportive enough, or if further assistance should be sought. If so, all the above-mentioned questions must be asked and the various factors taken into account.

Ideally, a crutch is chosen with its dispensability in mind. Any addictive substances such as repeat prescriptions, cigarettes, alcohol, some prescribed and many non-prescribed drugs undermine your coping skills and therefore your sense of self-worth, independence and creativity.

To return to my original analogy (that of the need for crutches when a leg is broken): if you were to continue to use crutches after the bone had knit, not only would you not know that healing was complete, but the muscles of your leg would atrophy, bringing new problems.

So too, over-reliance upon crutches in grief does not allow you to "find your own feet" and discover new strengths and zest for living.

3. Relaxation and pain meditation

When relaxation, a valuable self-help technique, is combined with meditation, release of tension and control of distressing emotional symptoms of grief are possible. Many types of physical pain are also responsive to these means.

Under prolonged stress your body experiences physiological changes: the initial fight or flight response to a threat results in increased rate of breathing, sympathetic nervous system activity, body metabolism, heart rate and blood pressure, and blood flow to the muscles in anticipation of protective action.

When stress is prolonged, as in grief, many of these changes settle into an established pattern and can lead to illness or dis-ease.

Being bereaved, you have been exposed to enough deprivation; you do not want to add loss of health to your troubles. The pain you feel, the resultant suffering, your health and well-being can all be positively influenced by relaxation and meditation.

Before I explain these techniques, I want to share with you a few comments by Hans Selye (1976:422) on sleep:

"The stress of a day of hard work can make you sleep like a log or it can keep you awake all night. This sounds contradictory, but if you come to analyze the work that helps you to sleep and the work that keeps you awake, there is a difference: Muscular activity or mental work which leads to a definite solution prepares you for rest and sleep; but intellectual efforts which set up self-maintaining tensions keep you awake."

Grief is, for a prolonged period, a self-maintaining tension until it is worked with (processed) and begins to subside. Selye goes on to say that "it is during the whole day that you must prepare your dreams". In other words, your sleep depends upon how you have spent your day.

The fact that you are grieving does not mean that you are powerless to help yourself. You can choose techniques found to be beneficial in helping you to get adequate rest and to relax.

As Herbert Bension in *The relaxation response* (1977:78) says, there are *four basic requirements* which facilitate relaxation and meditation:

☐ A quiet environment. Do not settle down near a telephone.
☐ An object to dwell upon. This may be your breathing, a flower in your mind's eye, a candle, repetition of a sound.
☐ A passive attitude. This means clearing the mind of thoughts, distractions.
☐ A comfortable position. If you wish to sleep, lying down is the obvious choice, but if you want to remain alert whilst lessening stress and quieting anxiety, sitting comfortably and well-supported (preferably with limbs uncrossed) is ideal.

Let us start with one of the simplest relaxation exercises which is easy to learn and very useful in that it can be used anywhere, anytime and by anyone. Spending ten minutes once or twice a day on this exercise, or even five minutes, is beneficial.

It works on the principle of relaxing the body and the mind, which is continuously and gently involved, and therefore controlled. You will find, as you become increasingly relaxed, that your breathing becomes slower, your body feels heavier and you have an expanding sense of inner quietness.

Having chosen a quiet environment and a comfortable position, close your eyes. Attend to your breathing: each time you inhale you will say "in" and on each exhalation you will say "out".

Quietly pay attention to your breath as it enters and leaves your body at its own natural pace. If any other thoughts come into your mind, don't tense up with annoyance; just let them go by like fish swimming in an aquarium and focus your attention back on your breathing.

Try it now: As you breathe in say "in", and as you breathe out, "out": in and out, easily and gently, at your own pace; in and out, in and out. Allow your limbs to feel heavier; resting; in and out, in and out. Your breathing will become slower and you will be comforted by the gentle rocking motion that you experience as you watch your breath go in and out. Take your time and gently allow all thoughts and tension to float away.

Lovingly allow yourself this time of peaceful relaxation, and continue for as long as you wish. Come out of it very gently, slowly opening your eyes and waiting a little while before you get up. No alarm clocks, no leaping to your feet; a gentle, slow return to daily activity, carrying the sense of relaxation with you.

The principle behind the pain meditation (based on one of Stephen Levine's, 1982:134) is that when in pain we tense up, tend to isolate the area affected, and reject the discomfort. In a sense we clench a fist around the pain to prevent it from spreading, yet by doing so we intensify the sensation. We tend to feel invaded by it and that we must be rid of it as soon as possible.

Emotional pain expresses itself physically: usually in the throat – that clenched up, closed feeling – the chest, solar plexus area in the midriff, or in the stomach.

The pain meditation uses guided imagery to release the tension in both mind and body and thus relieve the symptoms of distress.

Let us share an experience that can ease your pain. If you are very tense you may begin with the relaxation technique described above. You will then find it easier to settle into the meditation.

Close your eyes and turn your attention inwards. Focus on your pain. Can you feel that tight knot inside? Imagine that the muscles which are clenched in that area are a closed fist. Begin to open it; uncurl the fingers; release the tightness. Allow the pain to float there; no resistance to it, no desire to be rid of it; just permitting it to be there as you gently and lovingly open that fist, softening the muscles all around the pain.

Picture the muscles softening, the tight fist opening, the fingers unfurling. Let the pain simply float there; no trying to get rid of it; no trying to isolate it; just softening, progressively softening the muscles around it. Take your time. Feel the release; allow the pain the space in which to float. Just allow it; not judging nor rejecting. Keep softening and relaxing, slowly softening and relaxing, allowing space as you begin to realise that you are greater than your pain, that you can gently and caringly relax, become spacious, and let the pain float freely within. Stay for a while with this new experience.

When you are ready, bring your attention back to the present and gradually open your eyes, readying yourself to return to your activities. Carry within you the comfort you have gained.

As you release tension by ceasing to resist, and you permit the feelings to be there as a natural part of your experience of bereavement, you are no longer a victim of your pain. You now know that you do have a measure of control, that you can choose to deal with it and that you are able to significantly reduce its intensity.

(My relaxation and pain meditation audiotapes can be bought from the Head Office of The Compassionate Friends, PO Box 46305, Orange Grove 2119, Johannesburg. Telephone (011) 728-4451.)

4. Timing, process and change

Life is a process and change is constantly taking place both within and around you. It is useful, therefore, to pay attention to the cycles of ebb and flow. It is through patience and inner stillness that your sense of natural rhythms will develop. And it is only when quiet that you can perceive the subtler aspects of that which you already recognise.

Greater understanding of life's processes brings an increased sense of security during the unfamiliarity of the grief experience. It is important to realise this because bereaved people are so frequently told they must be patient. Beset by so much pain, it is hard to be anything but impatient.

Bear in mind that whatever phase you are struggling with will be resolved and give way to a new one. This in turn will alter because each is a step in the healing process. Perhaps, realising this, you will be able to relax a little and trust that your recovery is part of the natural cycle and will take place.

Everything has its season: early on in the grieving process it seems not only impossible to ever feel whole again, but inappropriate, disloyal. As time passes perspectives alter and you long for relief from pain. That which you feel unable to deal with now will become manageable. The process of change is kind, facilitative and trustworthy as an ever-present ally.

Thus when you feel out of step, with trust and the wisdom not to try to force the pace (for cycles have their own rhythm) you can allow change to follow its own pattern knowing that however confused and desperate you feel, the creative, healing life process is at work.

5. Pining is not forever

The definition of pining in *The Concise Oxford Dictionary* is "To languish or waste away from grief". Such helpless passivity! Pining is yearning for your child, the acute need that makes you listen for his/her voice or homecoming, search the rooms of your home, faces in a crowd, the passing cars to find him/her. The disbelief so common after a tragedy is related to this desperation: you pine so for your beloved son or daughter that it seems as if it simply cannot be true that s/he died.

It is natural to yearn for one you love and are separated from. You are not alone: your feelings and difficulties are shared by other bereaved parents. There should however come a time when passive grieving is replaced by active self-help. Otherwise you could "languish or waste away from grief".

So let us take a look at *three* ways of working with pining that will lead to healing:

● *Releasing emotional pain*
So often pining is not expressed. "I shouldn't still be feeling this way", or "Let me get on and help others, then I won't hurt so much", or "If I work myself to a standstill I won't feel the pain and I'll sleep at night" . . . and so on. There are endless rationalisations that parents can and do make that seem easier than the inner wrench of pining. But nothing is as effective as direct release of feelings.

Cry, be angry, talk it out, use appropriate physical means – you will need to do so repeatedly. Have compassion for yourself. Be as generous to yourself in the interests of your own healing as you would be to someone else in pain.

A further caution: many bereaved parents find it easier to care for others than for themselves. They use their concern as a distraction from their own anguish. When the constant bypassing of personal pain becomes habitual they find that they are in trouble. Their own grief demands their attention and there is simply not enough energy left with which to block it anymore whilst trying to comfort others. A sense of being overwhelmed is very frightening. Take care of yourself first; then help others if you wish to.

● *Setting appropriate goals*
This is an act of will – the opposite of passivity. Goal-setting signifies a decision to survive, to keep going and later on to find life meaningful again. The style in which you deal with your grief and bring about your healing is a very personal matter. For quite a time after a loss goals need to be simple, small, so that you can achieve them without too much difficulty. As you have these victories you gradually regain the sense of competence eroded by grief and this gives you courage.

● *Finding a context of meaning*
If you allow tragedy and pain to be ends in themselves and to colour your view of life, you are negating your ability to transcend these challenges. You deny yourself the opportunity to grow in understanding and to be enriched by remaining creatively open. Searching for new views, fresh approaches to the significance of life and to each person's relevance as a part of it can be rewarding indeed. Whether religion, philosophy, your own spirituality, or plain home-spun common sense is the source from which you draw meaning, all that matters is that it leads to inner peace and enables you to make what you wish of your life.

I want to emphasise that not one of these ways of working with pining replaces any other. The first, releasing emotional pain, takes care of your feelings. The second, setting appropriate goals, is constructive thinking and should include the physical needs that must be met. The third, finding meaning, is a form of spiritual self-care. Thus, although you will bear the scars of loss, for healing to take place at all levels of your being, attention must be paid to all three.

6. What does "letting go" mean to you?

Have you been told that you must let go of your child now that s/he has gone? Or that you are to let go of your grief? How do you feel about these recommendations? Perhaps you are wanting to do some releasing. A look at some aspects both of letting go and of holding on may help you to clarify your thoughts.

• Seven aspects of letting go
☐ Letting go of self-control: giving vent to feelings
This may be most necessary and will afford great relief. Healthy expression of your feelings is essential if you are to work through grief and find peace. Choose ways and times that suit you and allow yourself the healing that release of emotion brings.

If letting go of your self-control seems threatening, you are probably scared that you could be overwhelmed by pain, anger or perhaps guilt, and that you may not be able to stop crying or screaming. Maybe you are afraid you could become violent or self-destructive. You can make your fear work for you: it ensures that you proceed cautiously, so in a sense it is your safeguard. Trust your inner warnings to set the pace and let your feelings find expression bit by bit. You will gain assurance as you find that, taken slowly, they do not overwhelm you or others.

If fear is immobilising you, seek professional help so that you have that added security, guidance and support.

☐ Letting go of anger: renouncing it
This is another phase and a very different response. There may come a time when, because its cause cannot be removed and nothing more can be done to appease anger, you need to take a deliberate decision to relinquish it. It is like a fire: burning with great heat and then dying down if not replenished – but easily rekindled. The active resolution to let it go is akin to stamping it out, and is wisely taken when it is recognised that continuing aggression is held at the cost of health and general wellbeing. When you realise that even after a great loss life is worth living, you will find it possible to renounce anger.

☐ Letting go of relationships that seem too demanding
Perhaps your spouse, children, a parent, or other people seem to overburden you at present. Maybe all you want now is to be left alone to grieve without any demands, responsibilities, or advice. Use an imaginary "time-telescope" (mounted upon your life-experience) to help look ahead and sort out your priorities. You will see that grief does subside and life again becomes meaningful. You will find that your relationships can regain their previous value and significance, they may even be enriched. Surely your long-term needs are to avoid further loss? To reject relationships now, whilst mourning affects your judgement, is most unwise. Communicate your needs and feelings to someone who can help you to manage them; you will feel relieved.

☐ *Letting go of life: suicidal thoughts*
After the death of a child most parents have suicidal thoughts. It can be very frightening to feel so desperate, but death sometimes seems to offer longed-for release. Such thoughts may be accompanied by fear that you are losing your mind. All these are normal reactions to intense pain: bereaved parents from time immemorial have experienced what you are going through. Do not let go of life. Take only one minute at a time when it is hard to hold on. You can manage one minute, and the next, and the next; each a victory.

If enduring grief seems too much to bear, ask for help. It takes courage and effort but sharing your pain brings relief. You and your family must be spared another tragedy.

☐ *Letting go of hopes and dreams – your child's future*
The death of a child is, in a sense, a multiple loss. You have to give up your plans and ambitions for his/her future, and the opportunity to participate in his/her life. Perhaps you felt safe in the knowledge that your son/daughter would take care of you in your old age. Some parents feel the greatest loss is the opportunity their child had to make his/her mark in the world, whilst others grieve the loss of future grandchildren.

All this you must let go if it is not continuously to torture you. The process of relinquishing imaginings (for the future is not real until it becomes the present) is a slow but necessary one; we are not able to deal successfully with fantasy. Your child has a new present, a spiritual reality. Trust that all is well and taken care of. Turn your attention to your life and the value of making the now as meaningful as possible.

☐ *Letting go of your child*
When you decide to give away a treasured item you can let it go, perhaps with joy in the giving, maybe with regret. But when that treasure is taken without your permission you will probably cling to it or try to get it back again.

Although your children are not your possessions, when taken from you your natural response is to resist their going. This resistance has many forms: disbelief, denial, anger, clutching, searching . . . Letting go of your child seems outrageously inappropriate. But it is only when you begin to relax your grasp that you find out that in the essential sense your child is part of you and can never be lost. There is then no further need to hold on other than by cherishing his/her memory and presence with you. How reassuring that realisation is.

☐ *Letting go and letting God*
Some bereaved parents reach a point at which they are prepared to let go and allow God to take over. This may be just passivity, resignation, which can in time be changed into acceptance with the willing participation of the mourner. On the other hand it may represent a deepening faith, a trust which brings inner quiet, renewed strength and understanding.

● **Four aspects of holding on**
☐ *Holding on to the past by living in it*
Life is a process and requires us to keep moving with it. Choosing to remain behind, attached to the past, leaves you increasingly isolated, out of step with people and events. Your child must journey on and so must you. Strength and courage are provided for the way: recovery from grief through the ages is proof of this. If you feel that you do not have the energy to make the effort required, ask for the assistance of a therapist or counsellor. Medical or homeopathic treatment may also give you considerable aid.

☐ *Holding on by shrining*
Shrining is the extreme form of not wanting your child's room to be altered in any way, or his/her possessions to be touched. Often parents feel unwilling to make any changes for quite a time after the death. There is, understandably, a high level of sensitivity in relation to your child's absence. But when resistance to anything being moved continues, and the room is kept exactly as though the child is about to return, his/her presence is being held on to. This interferes with the natural process of grieving because it is unrealistic – a denial of the death. You do have to grieve in your own style and at the pace that is right for you, but it is important that no pattern becomes fixed. Each phase must be allowed to give way to the next and will naturally do so as long as you do not refuse to let it. Trust that readiness will come, for with your willingness to let it, it will.

☐ *Holding on through spiritualism*
I see the desire to consult spiritualists as symptomatic of the urge to keep your child close. The need to receive some message, some reassurance that he/she is alright is based upon the difficulty experienced in giving up the nurturant, protective role. As long as it is held onto, little progress can be made towards grief resolution. Giving

31

thought to having faith in the wellbeing of your child may help you to trust in God's care and find peace.

☐ *Holding on to surviving children: limiting independence*
Bereaved parents understandably become over-protective towards their surviving children for quite a while after the death. Having lost one child you become so afraid of any further loss that over-compensation in the interests of safety becomes a natural response. As a rule they object to having new restrictions placed upon their independence. The best way of dealing with the resultant friction is to explain your feelings, listen to your children's point of view and come to a mutually agreed-upon compromise. In time your sense of insecurity will fade and you will regain your equilibrium.

7. Extended grief

In life there are relationships and circumstances. Within them there is free choice as to whether or not and how to relate, respond and act.

Grief is a way of responding to loss and within that situation you have choices to make. What is your attitude to life going to be now that your child has died? You must choose whether to work towards recovery, understanding and growth, settle for resignation or extend the grieving period with no limits set. Whether your decisions are conscious or not, there are always reasons for them.

During mourning initially you hold on to your child in an attempt to prevent his/her departure. If the grief process progresses normally you gradually proceed, during the first year of loss, to experience lessening intensity of pain and less frequent, shorter periods of manifest grief. This happens because the perceived absence of your child is being accepted. This continues into the second year with recovery becoming more and more evident as active involvement in an increasingly satisfying life grows. As the intention to hold on to the child relaxes and attention is turned to the living, the "lost" one is found to be safe within the heart.

In extended grief the healing experience is forgone. Prolonged grief is acute grief that lasts until it becomes chronic. A style of living develops wherein all relationships and events are seen through the lens of loss. The insistence upon remaining inconsolable is destructive to family and other interactions. It contributes to deep unhappiness which feeds upon itself. Even though largely subconscious, the reasons for such a choice must be tackled if the problem is to be resolved.

- **What are the reasons that make non-relinquishment of grief patterns preferable to recovery?**

☐ It may be that suffering is perceived as the *only loyal behaviour*: that to recover is to forget. There is a fearfulness, a complication in the relationship that pre-dates the death.

☐ Perhaps the child was always a disappointment. After the loss there may be *compensation for a less than fulfilling relationship by idealization* and by extended grief for a fantasized close bond. There is a sense of shame. If the alliance between you and your child was not healthy, the grieving will not be healthy either.

☐ The pain of what might have been is often so intense that *anger* and sometimes *self-blame* take over and may be repressed. They extend grief in their mode: the world is dismissed in anger or with wringing of hands.

☐ Where a relationship with a child has been normal, idealization after the death may occur as a form of *holding on*. The deceased is remembered as perfect and the grief can only be partially worked through. The rest of the children seem, by comparison, imperfect and of little consolation. Their feelings of hostility, jealousy, and deprivation bode ill for family interactions.

☐ Sometimes parents have an *ambivalent relationship* with a child. There has been love but also great frustration and the occasional wish that this child was not a member of the family. There may have been demands that s/he meet your needs by being different. After that child's demise, and particularly if either of you was implicated in the death (eg. driving the car when s/he was killed) extended grief may result. There is a feeling of great remorse and of having been cheated. S/he has had the last word.

☐ The importance of not having been able to prevent a death, particularly when negligence has been a factor, can engender such *rage and determination to see that it will never happen again* that in the crusade healing is sacrificed. When a parent thinks he is to blame for what has occurred the resultant self-accusation and remorse is hard to let go of. In such cases it is imperative that you be prepared to take an honest look at your family members to see what your militant self-condemnation is doing to them. Loss compounds loss if recovery is disallowed.

☐ Extended grief can relate to the *significance of your child* for you. For example: when a marriage has been unfulfilling and either parent (more commonly the mother) has turned to the opposite-gender child for the satisfaction of (other than sexual) unmet needs and that child dies, the loss is compounded and grieving is complicated. Another example relates to role-reversal: you may have become dependent upon the child in some way(s) and upon his/her death are left feeling additionally vulnerable, destitute, deserted.

☐ Some people define themselves in terms of their relationship with their children. They live vicariously through them and after the death find it *difficult to redefine themselves* and still find life worth living.

These are some of the more common situations in which extended mourning can occur.

The advantages to you lie in the altered and preferred view the world is shown of both you and your child; the (distorted) picture of loyalty and closeness; the lessening of guilt through self-punishment; retaliation and revenge towards existing unsatisfactory relationships; attention gained and the concern and reassurance expressed; and when idealization is extreme the guilt engendered in other family members serves to prove your point that the deceased child was the perfect one. In such cases you require professional help to enable you to resolve your difficulties. The more entrenched you are in them the more unwilling to be counselled you are likely to be. The level of your enmeshment is directly related to your need for your grief. It is only when you can be brought to see at what cost both to yourself and your family your choice of coping is (and that there is a viable alternative with equal if not greater benefits) that you will be prepared to give up old patterns.

A role other than "mourner" must become more desirable, for only then will bonds become healthier.

8. Dealing with your grief

The subject of dealing with grief can be divided into two categories:
Dealing with new grief
Dealing with ongoing grief.

● *Dealing with new grief*

☐ Initially you will be experiencing shock and a resultant sense of unreality. You know something terrible has happened yet it cannot be . . . You are not able to take in what is being said and yet there is a sharp clarity . . . Impressions are intensified and within you a knot of grief makes you want to escape this nightmare, to be woken up and know what cannot be true is indeed not true.

The numbing shock is nature's tranquillizer. You cannot avoid the circumstance you find yourself in, but you do have built-in protective responses which are sub-consciously mobilized when necessary, to protect your sanity, and set the pace and (to some extent) the style of your grieving. We each know, deep within us, how much we can cope with. Trust, then, and listen to your inner sense of what is right for you in the days ahead.

☐ Your mourning is an appropriate process which will become one of rehabilitation. The range and intensity of your feelings may be frightening, but remember – you are not given more to bear than you are able to cope with. It is up to you to make the choice to come through, to heal and to find life meaningful again.

☐ *Deal with self-blame and a sense of guilt* if they are troubling you. Understand the difference between them, and between realistic and unrealistic guilt. (There is a section on p. 45 that will help you to gain perspective.)

☐ *Anger* is commonly felt during bereavement and is a complicated issue. (The subject is addressed on p. 42).

☐ Idealizing a child who died seems to be a natural response to a sense of bereftness; s/he is being seen as "larger than life" to compensate for your loss. This becomes a comfort and emphasises the validity of your longing and despair. But if you are to heal *idealization* must become *realisation* as you remember him/her as a fully human, real and fallible person. Any aspect (such as weakness, for instance), that you do not recall and mourn as a part of your child, leaves your grief-work incomplete. You are not being disloyal: pedestals are not for real people, and your child was and is real.

☐ *Break ongoing silence* about the death of your child and your feelings, and between you and your family members, your friends or colleagues. The loss is a fact and needs to be recognised in ways that reassure you that your child and the family's grief are important. It may be difficult to open up so painful a subject, however much you want to talk about your son or daughter, but you are well advised to keep trying to open communication channels.

Even though you may feel irritable with or critical of your friends (there is so much impatience in grief) *keep an open mind and heart to supportive people.* Sharing heals and new or deepened friendships develop. There will be some who avoid you and you may find this hurtful and get angry. Please read the fuller discussion on friends on p. 96.

● *Dealing with ongoing grief*

☐ If you are troubled by a repetitive "if only . . ." thought pattern, *recognise that regrets lead nowhere.* The clock cannot be turned back – but the present is important. What have you learned that you can make creatively useful? How can you use this opportunity to change your behaviour, outlook, expectations . . . or whatever it was that you so wish had been different? For instance, would developing more confidence in your parenting skills be useful? Perhaps it was something that could not, under the circumstances, have been any other way. If so, the regrets are using up precious energy to no avail. (The section on self-blame, p. 45 may help you with this.) Because the "if only's" can become a habit, a useful technique is to distract yourself whenever the chorus begins. Starved of attention it cannot survive.

☐ To answer the repeatedly asked question, "How many children do you have?" presents a difficulty for most bereaved parents. Your children are always yours, wherever they may be. You do not cease being a parent even when an only child or all your children die. How you wish to reply will depend upon who is asking and how you feel at the particular moment. A helpful rule to apply relates to whether or not you are going to have further contact with the questioner. If not, the word "now" is useful: if you say, "I have two children now" you will not feel disloyal in not having mentioned your deceased child and you are probably discouraging further questions. But if you will be seeing more of that person get the issue out of the way by saying "I have two children but had three" followed by an indication of whether the conversation may continue or not.

☐ Plan *new ways in which to celebrate birthdays and holidays.* Changing old patterns can make difficult days much easier. Anticipating is harder than the actual living of the day when it arrives. (There are sections on celebrations on p. 59 and on coping with holidays on p. 58.)

☐ *Take up some new activity* as soon as you can motivate yourself to do so. Through writing, drawing or painting, pottery, gardening and jogging, you can deal with pent up feelings. Reading can offer insight and new perspectives. If you make positive use of it, keeping a journal or making a scrapbook can be therapeutic.

☐ If you feel ready and so inclined, you may be considering trying to *meet the needs of other troubled people* – other bereaved parents, for example. Please take care that you are not blocking your own grief thereby. If you can meet your needs and theirs, it becomes a form of self-care and that is of great value. But if you find that you are using their troubles to escape your own pain, you are delaying your recovery.

☐ A great loss brings much confusion in its wake as old priorities lose their relevance and new ones replace them. Spend time *clarifying your values* – not "shoulds" and "oughts", but what is right for you – so that your inner experience of being changed by a death does not leave you in limbo, wondering who you are.

☐ It is what you do with your grief that determines what the outcome will be. Maybe this is a time in which you could *develop your faith*. Having faith means, amongst other things, not having to have the answers to every question. But asking the questions can lead you forward to new realisations. (There is a further discussion of this on p. 53.)

9. Grief and growth

Grief is the natural response to loss. As you go through the process, rehabilitation is taking place. It is up to you what the outcome will be. You can choose to grow, to be what Judy Tatelbaum calls a "creative survivor".

In her book *The courage to grieve* (1981: 83) she says that how you help yourself through mourning very much depends on your own self-support, that of your environment and your belief system. She also says that to become a creative survivor and to enhance the quality of your life you must make full use of all the backing available.

It does take courage to grieve, to not escape the pain and the tears. Blocking in one way or another is so much easier. You grow through experiencing your loss, through enduring the despair, loneliness and hurt. How many of you, if asked before your child died whether you would be able to cope would have said "yes"? You find you are given strength and that is encouraging.

Self-support is a form of *self-love*. Loving yourself means comforting yourself, accepting your feelings, attending to your various needs and allowing yourself your own timing in which to recover.

What else does *being self-supportive* during grief mean? It means *giving yourself permission* to feel and to do what seems best for you. No guilt or self-condemnation; just loving kindness. What you would offer another mourner you offer yourself.

This may entail being more active or quiet than usual; sharing feelings more or being more contemplative; getting sufficient rest; perhaps going for long walks or taking comforting hot baths; stretching exercises; listening to music . . . whatever is healing for you.

Environmental support might be family, friends, a pet, colleagues; perhaps professionals such as your doctor, clergyman, lawyer or a counsellor. Groups such as The Compassionate Friends can offer invaluable assistance. There are activities which you may find distracting or that relax, stimulate, interest, or enrich you. Maybe you want to travel, to attend art classes . . . The more appropriate the people and ventures (whether active or passive) that you have in your life, the more useful your environmental support system.

Your *belief system* might afford you great comfort and can be fertile ground for your further development. The meanings you ascribe to life, suffering, death, the universe and God affect the ways in which you respond to pain and loss. For example, people who accept pain as a part of growth find their belief to be supportive and useful during their time of transition.

Some of you may be resisting with questions such as, "Why should I grow through all this? How can I gain through my child's death, get anything positive out of such a loss? What sort of a parent would want to develop through grief?" In response I ask: If you had died and your child had lived, would you have wanted him/her to be able to grow through the experience, or to remain for years trussed up in sorrow? What would your child want for you?

The choice lies between having your energy bound into depression, or gradually re-emerging to make the most of life. The creative choice is not disloyal. It does not mean forgetting. You do your child honour by living his/her essence or special attributes that can in time come to expression through you.

10. Resignation and acceptance

Resignation is an aspect of depression – the helpless shrug, the view that "there is nothing I can do: I am stuck with this". It is a fearful, passive desperation in which many people live their lives.

The original meaning of acceptance was love. It means to be in agreement with, to consent to receive, to allow the truth of . . . This "allowing the truth of" is done through the heart not the mind. To reach acceptance it is necessary to learn to trust the integrity of the pain (which is its appropriateness in the face of loss). Rather than holding it at bay, allow the grief to be experienced while recognising it as part of a creative process.

As always, there is some measure of choice available to you as to what you do with your grief. You can resign yourself, having decided that you have no option, or you can choose active stillness, an opening of the heart to all the moments of pain, consenting to the truth of it and allowing it to carry you within to the inner place of connection with those you love. Stephen Levine says in his valuable book *Who dies?* (1982: 88) ". . . it is our essential love that we experience when the grieving mind sinks into the ever-present heart."

Initially the pain of separation is in the mind, the thoughts, associa-tions and memories, the questioning, the recognition of grief. Later it moves into the heart and there finds an awareness of union rather than separation. The sense of vulnerability is strong because the heart is now open. But be consoled: it is now ready to learn the lessons of true compassion.

So I say to you: "You know your child cannot be taken from you in essence; s/he is indeed within your heart and is part of you." You will feel relieved and comforted when you realise this.

Active acceptance means that there has been movement away from concepts in the mind; an entering into the heart to experience the unity and regeneration of what has seemed to be a lost relationship. Remem-ber: acceptance means love, and to consent to receive.

11. Communicating is essential

Shakespeare has Macbeth say: "Give sorrow words. The grief that does not speak whispers the o'erfraught heart and bids it break."

How wise! Good communication is particularly important whilst grieving because of the confused feelings, heightened sensitivity and vulnerability of all the family members.

I define good communication in this context as a sharing (preferably mutual) that:

- [ ] expresses and clarifies thoughts and feelings thereby increasing understanding;
- [ ] is supportive, consoling, and facilitates both healing and growth;
- [ ] brings the communicants closer by strengthening marital and other family bonds.

After a loss meaningful communication seems to peter out in most families. What hinders it just when it is so important? It may be useful to try and answer this question by taking a look at personal and then social issues. Hopefully, understanding what underlies your particular difficulty may help you to resolve it.

- **Personal inhibitors of communication**
  - [ ] A sorrow and pain that may at times be deeper than you can express
  - [ ] An immobilising sense of futility, impotence . . .
  - [ ] A desire for privacy and not to have your grief taken away . . .
  - [ ] Fearfulness: that you cannot cope, your thoughts and feelings are not normal, you will go mad, that if you release your grief there will be no holding you . . .
  - [ ] A sense of self-blame and/or guilt
  - [ ] Family conditioning, shyness, a withdrawal that is natural to you, inarticulateness
  - [ ] Protectiveness of other family members
  - [ ] The belief that no-one can understand . . . or that men and women grieve differently and so cannot help one another
  - [ ] The belief that the other parent cares less than you do (this will arouse antagonism – never conducive to sharing)
  - [ ] Unmet needs. These may be physical, emotional . . .
  - [ ] Anger. A tight control may be being kept so that it does not get out of hand. Anger is generally seen as destructive rather than as a useful form of energy.

- **Social inhibitors of communication**
  - ☐ Expression of feeling is not generally encouraged in our society
  - ☐ The cruel dictum "Big boys don't cry" has all too frequently conditioned men not to allow themselves the healing comfort of tears
  - ☐ A man's role of supporting his family carries these two expectations
    - ☐ to be self-contained enough to be able to assist them
    - ☐ to carry on with business as usual. You must earn a living. To do so means submerging the pain, and this can become habitual
  - ☐ Little understanding of how different individual grieving can be, and what help children require (there is a section on siblings' grief that follows this one)
  - ☐ A taboo, a carry-over from the past, which makes communication difficult, e.g. with regard to suicide
  - ☐ Lack of a supportive network when you are living at a distance from family and friends, or when you do not avail yourselves of what is offered.

Non-communication leads to misunderstandings, discord, alienation, isolation, and loneliness. In addition, anger, depression, gradual estrangement, and possibly a turning elsewhere for comfort can result. I want to underline how essential it is to communicate. However difficult it may be, the risks of avoidance are great, and you have all suffered enough.

- **How can communication be improved?**

There is no quick-fix; patterns generally do not change very easily. So *consistent hard work* is required not to let the opportunities for sharing words, tears, hugs slip by unused. Sometimes sorrow *is* too deep for expression, but only at times. Grief ebbs and flows and so there are low tides when it is easier to talk. When words do not come, being held or crying together speak volumes. Do not waste these moments; they are precious. Be patient with one another and offer encouragement.

Perhaps the most important thing of all, realising how much is at stake, is to want to improve matters.

The listings above show that there are a number of *assumptions* that can underlie non- or even poor communication. Do you make any of these? Test yourself now. For instance:

☐ "My husband does not care as much as I do." Perhaps he does, but he does not show it as you do. Try to talk about it and allow your different styles. It could bring you closer to one another.

☐ "It's not manly to cry." (Many men and women believe this.) It is natural to cry. It brings relief and healing and is appropriate when a child dies. But learned patterns interfere with many men's inner permission. It is a detrimental stereotype that should be let go of.

☐ "I must protect my wife" may isolate her. Talk about it and find out what her needs are. Go through the lists together and see if you can improve communication. Sustained effort to do so, to understand the process of grief and what you can expect, will help. (See "The grief experience" on p. 147). It will give you insight into what you are going through, show that your reactions are normal, and perhaps assist you to feel less confused. All this will make communicating easier. Try to be less fearful of opening up to each other's pain; isolation and exclusion are far more frightening.

If there are times when you cannot cry or scream and you need to, do so in your head. It is effective. Sometimes writing things down can replace speaking about them, but do not let notes or letters displace the two-way sharing of talking and being heard, listening and responding.

But it does not have to take two to communicate; if a family member is finding it difficult, one person can improve interaction, so take heart!

Finally, it can be most comforting and valuable to communicate with your deceased child, holding him/her in your mind's eye and saying all the things you wish you had been able to. It is never too late to express your love, longing and regrets. Perhaps messages of or requests for forgiveness will bring you peace. When people are bonded closely the lines of discourse are open. As you speak to your child you will probably know exactly what s/he would want to reply to you.

12. Anger

Before discussing anger I want to say to anyone who is not feeling angry that:

☐ it is so common in grief that it is almost expected of the bereaved. Nevertheless it may just not be relevant for you, and circumstances vary as do the responses to them;

☐ even though you do not experience it you may in fact be angry. Some people need "permission" before they can get in touch with so strong an emotion. Perhaps you feel it is wrong, or are afraid that if you do release it you will be overwhelmed. Be reassured that it is not wrong to respond to a loss with anger. You can choose how to express it and to what extent so that it will not demolish you or anyone else. When you find that you can release it a little at a time you will begin to trust yourself and your emotions.

Anger is a form of energy that is natural and understandable. The key to its management is acceptance without self-blame, and its appropriate expression. Held in it tends to backfire in irritable outbursts which do not resolve anything and can create difficulties. It also tends to turn inwards and become destructive to the person holding onto it. Repressed, it can lead to depression.

Anger needs an object. The person or situation chosen as target may be appropriate (e.g. if your child died through medical negligence and you are enraged with the doctors). Or you may be displacing the generalised fury at having lost your child onto someone innocent who then becomes a scapegoat. It is important to take responsibility for the way in which you express it and towards whom it is directed.

The range of anger's evidence is wide: frustration, irritability through outrage to frenzy.

Commonly it is directed at the person responsible for the death if it was by accident, your spouse, surviving child or children, other family members. Friends, colleagues, other parents who have all their children, the doctor, police, God, life in general, the grieving person him/herself, the deceased child, any or all can be the target. The energy has to go somewhere. Sometimes it is rational and sometimes irrational.

Feelings are not good or bad, but what you do with them is the issue that requires some control. Some parents do not want to be rid of their anger: they feel it is warranted, and in a sense a tribute to their child that his/her death arouses such strong emotion. Others wish for peace of mind and to be relieved of their ongoing hostility. Whether or not you want to hold onto these feelings, you do need someone with whom to share them. If you think that your choice has been irrational, unfair, you will probably want to redirect your rage. Some of it may be related to there not being anyone with whom you feel you can really talk about your child, your grief. Sharing feelings is a great help and needs to be done repeatedly with someone you can trust to understand and really listen.

Some parents, often fathers, prefer to deal with their anger in private rather than share their emotion with others. Each person must find the way that is right for him/her. Nevertheless, often what is done alone is desolate rather than creative, and not necessarily healing. The value of sharing lies both in the comfort found in communion with another person who cares, and in the perspective offered.

- **Ways of coping with anger** (You may want to add your own ideas)
  - [ ] Talk through and let go of past hostility that was not resolved and still troubles you. By association it feeds your present agitation.
  - [ ] If you are having difficulty with guilt about your anger with God, speak to a minister who can help you. Recognise that God can take your rage.
  - [ ] Fury against the individual who caused the death will have to be responsibly worked through and then consciously let go of when you feel ready. It does not just dissolve.
  - [ ] Discover whether anger with yourself is rational or irrational. If the latter, let it go. If the former, give deep consideration to repentance (if relevant) and self-forgiveness.
  - [ ] Seek help about animosity towards your spouse or surviving children because it can be damaging.
  - [ ] Anger towards your deceased child which continues for many months without lessening in intensity, could be talked through with someone who can help. It is enough to have lost your son or daughter; that child's value to you must not be negated as well. For you to recover from grief you need to have an acceptable memory of your loved child restored to you. Can you separate his/her *being* from the *doing*? You can still love someone whilst feeling furious or hurt by his/her behaviour.

    Perhaps you are angry that s/he got him/herself killed. However irrational, that stems from your love for your child. Talk to someone about it. It needs to be worked through.

    Practical, physical expression of hostility is satisfying. Beat pillows, stamp up and down, kick a ball, jog, dig in the garden until you are tired out, scream in the shower (the water running is an effective sound barrier), scream in your head, hurl a plastic

44

talc powder box into the bath, do tiring household chores like cleaning windows, wax stripping or sorting out the storeroom.

☐ Visualisation is effective for some people: in your mind's eye see the individual against whom you hold anger and do to him whatever brings you relief. You may have to repeat this exercise a number of times at intervals before a way is cleared for more rational thought.

If you intend using the visualisation technique it is essential that you accept the obligation to restrict this venting of fury to your imagination.

Remember: anger is energy, you have both a responsibility and a choice as to how you deal with it.

Forgiveness is dealt with later (on p. 48). Having released anger, you may feel the need to forgive yourself for the destructive thoughts you have had. All of this takes time but this is the first step towards forgiving others. By taking it you will feel relieved, lighter and freer.

13. Guilt and self-blame: a brief overview

A sense of guilt and self-blame are almost invariably present in mourners and must be confronted and dealt with. The importance of self-condemnation relates to its influence upon the rest of your life. Ongoing, it has a detrimental effect. You can choose not to live with it continuously.

It is generally thought that our conscience gives rise to feelings of guilt when we have not done as we ought. I want to suggest that conscience and guilt are opposite in origin. You have developed a conscience on the basis of the moral teaching that you have received. Having internalised it (i.e. having made it your own) your choice of action becomes an *inner* responsibility in each situation. Guilt, on the other hand, is from an *outer* source. It originates in the judgement by others, or your expectation of that external disapproval. It is the "you ought (not) to" and the "you should (not)" rather than the "I (do not) want to".

The relevance of this distinction lies in taking responsibility for your morality. It is up to you to right any wrongs that you can, and ask forgiveness for those you cannot. (This means recognising, if you are a Christian, that Christ takes on the wrongdoing of every individual that s/he is not able to put right.) The judgement by and censure of others is of no consequence. You do not have to assume guilt; your behaviour should be a matter of personal inner morality.

Having said that, I turn now to the self-blame with which the bereaved so frequently struggle.

It can be assessed on a continuum which ranges from minimal to obsessive. Rate your view of your blameworthiness (with regard to the circumstance that is troubling you) on a scale of 0-7 (0 = minimal). Then ask someone who knows you well to rate it without having first seen your assessment. The comparison may shed new light and put matters into better perspective.

What is being evaluated is your behaviour and its consequences (your view of which may or may not be correct), and not you yourself. This is a very important distinction and one that is seldom recognised. The issue of self-accusation, realistic or not, arises from your having judged *yourself* as having acted inadequately or wrongly – and not just the action that has not met your standards. You must not become identified with it. Because you are not your wrong-doing there is no need to think that you yourself are bad.

Mourners often hold on to self-blame. This is partly because it is sub-consciously seen as a link with the deceased; partly because of a deep sense of shame, usually accompanied by an ongoing need for punishment. To the extent that it is guilt taken within, it is destructive and interferes with healing.

What are you doing to yourself with self-censure? Distressing yourself, day and night; disturbing your metabolism; binding your energy (always in short supply anyway during grief); angering or depressing yourself. The list could continue. To deal with self-accusation first find out whether it is realistic or not. Having established that, take a look at what you can do about it.

● *Unrealistic and realistic self-blame*
Unrealistic self-blame has no foundation in reality. For example: it was not possible for you to be present at your child's death and yet you blame yourself. You maintain that you should have been there. Appropriate feelings might be anguish, a sense of being cheated perhaps, anger . . . there are a number of choices – but why blame? In the helpless impotence you experience when there is nothing that you can or could do to alter a situation, you come face to face with human limitation.

So often it is not possible to be in control, and that can be a frightening realisation. Working towards coming to terms with that will be of more value to you than focusing on unrealistic self-accusation. It is not realistic because you could have done nothing to change matters.

It is also important to take a look at the motivation behind the behaviour for which you censure yourself. If your underlying intention was honestly in the best interests of whoever was concerned, there is no need for self-blame. You may be upset at the outcome, but you did not intend to do wrong.

Realistic self-condemnation, on the other hand, relates to what reasonably should not have been done and was; or should have been done and was not – when you perceived it and it *was* within your power to have acted differently. Where an action or non-action has had an unfortunate result self-blame is useful only as a spur to taking right responsibility for it.

Holding on to self-censure is neither required nor healthy. It is detrimental to your sense of self-worth and therefore has a negative effect upon your relationships with others.

I want briefly to address those of you who feel that you are implicated in the death of your child. It may have been a drowning, a road accident, suicide . . ., whatever the cause. If you *are* bearing realistic self-blame it may well be that you do not intend to relinquish it. Many parents feel bound to do penance: unable to live with themselves unless they continue in their self-torture. I ask you, with respect for your decision, to remember that God is a God of compassion and that Christ takes upon Himself that which you can no longer alter. The time must come when you can feel that you have paid in full in suffering, are free to ask for forgiveness and to accept that it is given.

Before going on I will just make mention of "survivor guilt". This term describes the remorse felt at having outlived your child; the particular pain a parent, grandparent or sibling (amongst others) experience because they are still living and do not feel that they have the right to be. It is not for anyone to say when his time on earth is complete, whatever reversal there seems to be in the natural order of life. A positive response that you can make if plagued by survivor guilt is to accept the responsibility of making your life a tribute to your child's memory.

● *Responsibility, self-condemnation and release*
Bonds must not become bondage: be willing to relinquish your self-blame. Ways of resolving unrealistic self-accusation have been re-

ferred to already. What do you do when it is unresolved but realistic? It is essential that you take the decision to work with it if you do not wish to continue undermining yourself, destroying your peace of mind and delaying recovery from loss.

Responsibility has to do with response, and with ability. You have response-ability to recognise that you are human and fallible, and that you are not suffering for any wrongdoing. There are limits to what is appropriate and you do not have to play the role of Harsh God, committing yourself to endless penance for what has occurred.

You have a response-ability to talk out your self-censure; share your thoughts and feelings (perhaps repeatedly) so that you can experience acceptance, gain perspective and heal the memories. Speak to someone who understands and really listens.

For as long as you keep yourself on the treadmill of blame, you bind your family to your pain. In releasing yourself you release them. You also clear the way to a new, albeit changed, relationship with your deceased child.

How relevant to you is the response-ability you have to God or to Christ to align yourself with Him as He leads you from remorse to forgiveness, redemption and release from the bondage of self-accusation? What about the God-given response-ability you have to recover and lead a meaningful life once more? These questions relate to your willingness to relinquish self-blame. By being prepared to share your anguish and allow it to be stilled within you, you become the inner meeting place of pain and healing. Having experienced this, you will truly be in a position to be of help to others, and perhaps this is one of the meanings inherent in suffering.

14. Difficult relationships and forgiveness

Grief after the death of a child with whom you have had a difficult relationship can be complicated. The pain of loss is a mixture of hollow regret for what might have been – the opportunity for loving closeness lost – and an unease if not outright self-blame because nothing was resolved. There is likely to be anger too: with the child for having been so troublesome and with yourself and/or perhaps other family members for not having been able to relate differently to him/her.

As parents you are guardians of your children to protect and guide them through the early years. Each individual, child or adult, must find his/her own way of being by making choices, learning from mistakes and enjoying the victories. If you wish to clear the turbulence in your heart you must be prepared to realise that however your son/daughter behaved, it is only your response that you can work with. Recognise that doing and being are not the same. Whilst finding someone's behaviour (the doing) unacceptable, you can still accept the person (the being).

Perhaps the best way that I can help is by sharing a situation with you which I recently had to resolve: For years I have felt trapped in a distressing relationship with a family member. As a result I have carried retaliatory weapons of resentment and rejection. I have felt uncomfortable and therefore angry. But the trap was mine, not hers. Whilst she was dying, I was given the gift of time: time to look at the cost of my antagonism, of how it had reduced her worth in my eyes and how victimised I had become by my opinionated egoism. I was failing my own sense of integrity. It was in this honouring of what I value as my true self that the solution lay. It became imperative that I set my negative views aside and took a look at what I had hosted within myself for so long. The time had come for change.

These are the steps that took me beyond my difficulties:

- [ ] *I asked God for forgiveness.* It was painful, recognising how judgemental I had been and that I had been too arrogant to allow space for her expression of her spirit.
- [ ] *I accepted that forgiveness was granted me.* I had to forgive myself or useless self-condemnation would have interfered with what I still had to do.
- [ ] *I affirmed myself*, recognising that care and clarity were called for in this confrontation. Without my own permission, so to say, I would not have been able to acknowledge my own worth. And unless I could love myself I knew I could not love her, for envy gets in the way when we offer to another what we cannot accept for ourselves.
- [ ] *I opened myself to compassion* for both her and my human frailty, and took an honest look at what had made the relationship so complex. I consciously relaxed my hold upon the negativity, anger and hurt. Tears helped them to slide away and cleansed the wounds.
- [ ] I was then ready to go to her, to *tell* her all that I needed to and to ask her forgiveness. For the first time since she had become ill my pity became compassion, my love was released and I felt no more anger. From then on I sensed her closeness. Since her death I have experienced her essence as bonded with mine.

Before I took the responsibility of resolving our difficult relationship I would never have said that this experience was possible.

It is never too late to get in touch with love that is unhampered by negativity. It does not matter who has been mostly in the wrong. Be thankful that you can make the right choice and that you have the ability to release yourself, him/her and family from such bondage. Seek the essence of your son/daughter with all the love that is the truth of you, and be reunited. Talk to your child within your heart, that place of deep connection. When the difficulty in the relationship is resolved, you will know the blessed sense of healing.

15. Memories: their value

Memories span the gap between the past and the present. In an abstract though none-the-less real sense you can have your child with you by remembering. At the same time you are facilitating healing, for there is a proven link between recall and recovery from grief. The memories whether of happy, sad or just humdrum times, are special. Sometimes they bring a smile but, particularly in early bereavement, they can be so painful that you might want to block them out to escape the hurt. And yet the loss of your memories would leave a gap.

Amongst the most difficult to deal with are the sudden stabs of longing that catch you unawares when you see his/her favourite food in the supermarket, hear a remembered song on the radio . . . When this happens try to take some deep, slow breaths; that does help.

For some parents the pain relates to how little there is to remember: the stillbirth, for instance, leaves only memories of the pregnancy and perhaps of having held the baby for a brief span. (See section on stillbirth and neonatal death, p. 99.)

Although you may find the turbulent times with your child more distressing to remember than the contented ones, I must emphasise the importance of recalling the varied facets of your relationship without censorship. Naturally you will only allow recollection of the memories you can cope with; subconscious defences protect you from being overwhelmed. But blocking those that are "bad" leaves them unprocessed, stored, in a sense denied. Far better to remember and work with the associations by thinking or talking them through. You lessen the sorrow and also avoid putting your child on a pedestal.

When grieving we tend to close in on ourselves. (See the pain meditation on p. 23 to help you work with this.) Can you use the memories as a vent into your heart where the connectedness, the inseparability and comfort lie? They can take you there, such is their value and effectiveness. In time the pain of recall will fade; still later the sadness will recede and then your memories will bring you both solace and joy.

16. Setting goals

The more recent your loss the less you may be inclined towards setting goals. Just getting through a day can be so difficult that each one managed is a victory – and perhaps you feel that is enough. Nevertheless, aspiring to climb is to begin to build a ladder up from the depths.

I offer you a framework within which you can choose the steps that are right for you in the grieving process. To this end I have taken the concept of *reclaiming your power* from Christopher Spence (1986) and related it to bereavement.

It is normal for mourners to feel helpless for quite a while having been powerless to prevent the irreversibility of the physical fact of death. The unsettling features of grief compound the sense of impotence. Thus reasserting your strength is an antidote. It places you in a position of active effectiveness which proves that you are coping, and leads to healing.

The framework is made up of three broad categories which, as a bereavement counsellor, I have found need our attention. Your restorative goals will emerge from them:

● **Building a loving relationship with yourself**
This means recognising, however you are feeling now, that you are worthy, valuable and have both the right and the ability to choose to live meaningfully. Your grief must not displace you. Under normal circumstances your health reflects the extent to which you lovingly care for yourself.

A goal could therefore be to respond to your body and its needs and, in addition, to express emotions without reluctance or shame. Perhaps you think that you are strong and can "take it". Up to a point that may be true, but can you release it? Failing to take appropriate care of yourself when under prolonged stress is a form of self-abuse which is hardly consistent with self-love.

● **Counterbalancing a sense of isolation**
This involves building a sustaining affinity with yourself and putting

relationships with others onto the best possible footing. It means encouraging closer family bonds and warm friendships. It is enriching to establish links across any limiting boundaries such as age, gender, class, culture, religion and occupation.

In accepting such goals, can you see how you are reclaiming your power in most creative and generative ways?

Another means by which you can counterbalance the loneliness of grief is to meet your needs and those of appropriate others for physical closeness (the comfort of being held), and express your sexuality with loving acceptance and respect. Further, put affirmation of yourself and others into thoughts, words and actions. Spence (1986:42) says that the ratio of appreciation to criticism should be at least 10:1.

● *Refusing to limit your capacities*
Recognise your worth and agree to act in your own best interests. It means releasing your pain and accepting that in time your days will again contain happiness. It asks you to acknowledge that your life role is of value and that you bring a special quality to it. It also means staying in touch with your sense of integrity (grief can for a time be dislocating and distort perspective). Meeting the challenge of loss, which in essence is giving a creative answer to the question: "Will you be victor or victim?" is perhaps the crux of this whole issue of not allowing yourself to be diminished by death.

This may sound a tall order for mourners, but the lower your motivation and energy levels the greater your need for healing and restoration. To reclaim your power is to find life meaningful again. It is up to you to select the goal or goals that seem within your reach and therefore right for you. The climb back to effective living is not an easy one, but is well worthwhile.

17. Restoration

When your child dies the relationship you have had becomes a relationship with grief. The pain of loss is now associated with that child; indeed it fills all your thoughts of him/her. You may sub-consciously and loyally be holding on to your anguish as the connecting link between you. It is as if all that is left is to relate to that child through the pain of loss.

It is important to recognise that though the interaction between you must undergo certain changes, your grief is your response to his/her death and not a new relationship. For healing to take place restoration is necessary; your mourning will not be completed until it has occurred.

By restoration I mean that the child, although no longer physically present, is reinstated as part of the family circle. (In one sense past and present are inseparable.)

The emphasis then, rather than being on the gap s/he has left behind, can be on loving appreciation and thankfulness for him/her.

This change comes about, over time, through the recall and recounting of shared experiences. Memories bring about a realisation of the particular characteristics and significance of the relationship; when shared they emphasise its vitality.

Sometimes the nature or the cause of death has had the effect either of taking the child out of his/her family context, or of so overwhelming the mourners that grief seems to have greater density. As a result the child will seem even more remote.

An example of the first situation is a "public" death: the media, by emphasising newsworthy aspects and making them common knowledge, may leave the family feeling their privacy has been invaded and their child made public property.

In the second situation the cause of death carries particular horror: suicide, homicide . . .

In these cases restoration is particularly important and will need specific attention. (I have dealt with ways of facilitating it on p. 171 in the section for counsellors. You may find it helpful.)

The fact that restoration (in the sense that I use it) is possible, reassures us that essentially you do not lose your beloved child. In many ways your interconnectedness has a reality and an ongoing truth. The relationship now continues in another context. It is the grief response that interferes, blocking your experience of it. When the pain subsides you will find the closeness you yearned for.

It is natural to hold on to a loved one when you fear loss; it is when you begin to let go that you discover that your son/daughter is within your heart, a part of the family still, and you need hold on no longer. It is then that restoration has taken place.

18. Spiritual need

Bereaved parents repeatedly ask: "Why?" "Why did my child have to die?" "Why did it happen to us?" "Why when s/he had everything going for him/her?" "Why have children when you have to lose them . . .?" "Why did God do this to us?" and so on, ad infinitum.

Perhaps "why?" is the only question you can ask when your child has died. There are answers and there are no answers; the questioning helps you to vent your grief and anger and will in time bring you to a stage when it loses its sting.

It is part of your religious experience, however rejecting of Deity you feel. God can stand your rage. He understands, and can wait for your return. You may think that you are through with religion for all the help it has been in this time of need. You may be angry at being told that God can take it. You do not care whether He can or not. That is the way it is now, for you. The discomfort, perhaps a fearfulness that you may be unaware of beneath the anger and despair, might help you to alter that decision if you should become ready and needful to do so.

Struggle with the why, rail against fate, express whatever you need to offload; you will feel better for it. Change will come.

Meanwhile it may help to consider that God does not will children to die. He does not take, but He receives them. He has given life in abundance – and that must mean after-life as well as that lived here on earth. You want to know why He did not intercede and save your child if He is all-powerful and a loving God. I suggest that you spend time with your minister: some clarification and a great deal of comfort can be derived from such discussions and prayer.

Do not by-pass your spiritual need if you feel God has failed you. There is much to be explored and great wealth of spiritual newness and deepening that you have the opportunity to make yours. It is up to you, for both your own sake and your family's to creatively work with your questions. You can allow something meaningful to grow from and transform your tragedy: what a testimony of parental love!

How to cope . . .

B In specific situations

1. Grieving and driving

So often the subject of drinking and driving is addressed in the press and on television. What about grieving and driving? There are so many analogies. Which bereaved parent has not at some time been actively grieving whilst driving?

What does this mean? What are the implications and what can be done about it? Grief, somewhat like alcohol, clouds awareness, alters perceptiveness, and is distracting. Tears blur vision. Angry grief is also dangerous behind a steering wheel because it can become vengeful. Depression evokes that desolate feeling that nothing matters anymore – driving into a tree . . . speeding . . . nothing.

The implications are obvious: it is not safe to actively grieve and drive. Not for yourself, your family (whether or not they are in the car with you), nor for other road-users and pedestrians. Because your concentration and reaction times are affected by grief you are well-advised to drive more slowly and try to be extra-cautious.

How can you, as bereaved parent, take care? For some of you, time spent in your car is the only opportunity in the day to be alone – and so the tears come there. One answer is to cry before you have to leave: shut yourself in the bathroom for privacy and release the pent-up emotion that you are carrying within. Or perhaps you can hold your tears until you can park in some side road on the way and take time to cry before continuing? You must find appropriate ways in which you can take responsibility for safe driving.

The power of the engine is tempting when you are angry. It may seem to be a well-deserved relief to recklessly accelerate. Maybe your child was killed on the road: will it help to injure or cause another death?

The awful feeling that nothing matters is one of the hardest to combat. Most bereaved parents feel at one time or another that they would like to die and, coupled with the seeming meaninglessness of life, it is easy to get things out of perspective and drive carelessly.

Please remember that, whatever form of grief you are experiencing whilst driving, all your children would want you to be safe and would be horrified if they knew you might have or cause an accident.

2. "I should have been there"

One of the hardest things to live with is the pain of not having been with your child when s/he died. The parenting role is outraged at having been apart at such a crucial time.

How to cope with the "if only's", the regrets, the self-blame and sense of having been cheated; what to do with the anger and the pressing need for details so that at least by proxy you can share in your child's last moments? Having some answers will help you towards finding peace of mind.

Let us take them one by one:

● **The "if only's" and the regrets**
Through them you are trying to turn the clock back – a futile exercise. You will have to accept that it is not possible and that the regrets lead nowhere. This is difficult when you are bereft and angry. Facing the fact that you cannot reverse the loss is deeply painful but is part of grief-work and therefore a positive step. So do not let the "if only's" get a grip on your thoughts. To break the pattern, distract yourself when that chorus begins by doing something practical or creative that engages your attention. Relief from the treadmill of helplessness will sustain your new technique.

● **Feelings of self-accusation**
These are best dealt with by the *realisation* of the *fact* that the death took place whilst you were elsewhere, rather than the *ideal-isation* of what, in your view, *should* have been. It is natural for you to want to protect your child during any crisis and if you were not present you might tend to be self-condemnatory and feel cheated. Nevertheless you were not there and tormenting yourself helps neither you nor him/her. In addition, beware of thoughts and feelings that tell you that you ought to suffer and do not have the right to peace of mind. Unless your child's death was caused by your wilful negligence or attempt to murder, you do not carry the blame. Indeed you have a responsibility to recover for your own and your family's sake.

● *Anger is a potent form of energy*

It may be strongly felt as you consider the mode of death and your absence at the time. Perhaps some of it is directed at your child for having been killed. Your feelings, both rational and irrational, are understandable even if disturbing to you. You may be censuring yourself for some of them. Your impotence to alter the course of events brings an awareness that the control you thought you had is only relative. A sense of safety must be sought in terms of that reality rather than in fighting it. Vulnerability is a part of being human but so is the strength and courage to deal with it creatively.

Grief, anger and love are often found in partnership. You grieve because you love and do not want to let go, and you are angry because you love and are being asked to let go.

Express your anger in ways that harm no-one, and give expression to your love as well. Tell your child all the things that you wish you had said: say them holding him/her in your heart the while.

The pressing need for details of the death is felt (unless the circumstances were too shocking), because gaining information is an attempt to be with your child. Perhaps you are also feeling you have the right to know. If so, and you are unable to get the information, it is very necessary that you work through your anger to the point when you can let it go. It must not become damaging to you. (See this subject on p. 28.)

It may be important for you to know that when death is caused by a sudden impact or very frightening circumstance the shock anaesthetizes pain. If you have ever hit your thumb with a hammer you will have experienced that numbness for a time.

The transition through death to new life is not made alone. There is always spiritual help. Your child is in safe hands. The bond between you ensures that s/he knows that you would have wanted to be there. Of course you have the desperate wish that you could have prevented the death – yet you could not have. Who really knows why the circumstances were as they were? We cannot see how the pattern of life and death is woven, nor understand the timing.

Rather than investing in thoughts of your absence, you can think back to all the important moments in your child's life when you *were* present. If you do not want to continue to be anguished you are going to have to choose to relinquish the regrets. Allow an acceptance of all that has been right and precious in your relationship to fill that place of pain with good memories, gratitude and affirming love.

3. Christmas and other holidays

The festive season, when tinsel and excitement are in the air . . .
schools are closing for the holidays, plans are being made, the shopping rush and scramble is on. Many bereaved parents stand, cold
within and lonely in the midst of it all, wondering if it is possible to get
through this time without being emotionally torn apart and physically
totally drained.

Holiday times and festivals carry memories of past plans and celebrations that now, with a child missing, seem to heighten sensitivity to
the loss. They do get easier to handle as time goes on; the first ones are
always the hardest. Drawing from the experience of other bereaved
parents and tailoring these ideas to suit your own needs may prove
helpful.

First decide what your particular needs are and how best you, as a
family, can manage your grief. Caring for one another, and with
awareness of the spirit of the festival approaching, acknowledge and
accept your feelings.

You may have to give yourself and your children "permission" for
enjoyment, recognising that whilst there is so much sadness there can
be happy anticipation too. It is alright to laugh, to feel excited. There
is no need for any of you to feel guilty.

If it cannot yet be a joyful Chanukka, a merry Christmas or a happy
New Year, it can still be a time of giving thanks for your child, for
those present, for shared memories. It can be a time for banding together as a family and helping one another through; for even when it
feels as if life has stopped for all of you, it does go on and you are a part
of it.

So, in practical terms, set yourself attainable goals taking into account your energy level and vulnerability. As a family decide what you
want to do: for instance, which traditions do you wish to continue with
and which would make it easier if you were to change? Do not make
plans that will isolate you if you feel the need for company. Identify
your priorities and decide what you can manage.

Shopping may seem an insurmountable task: perhaps facing holiday
cooking, gift wrapping or other tasks leave you feeling overwrought. If
you have young children you may be wanting them to have a share in
Christmas festivities, yet feel unable to do anything about it.

Try to reduce pressure on yourself: make lists, share tasks that you
feel you cannot undertake alone with family members and friends.

Make your needs known and accept the help offered. It may be hard to make decisions. Turn to those who will understand and have helpful ideas (but do not be afraid to say "no" when you wish to). This is a time not only for giving, but also for receiving.

You may derive comfort from doing something for others: maybe to donate the money you would have spent on your child to a charity as a gift in his/her memory. Or to invite someone who is alone to spend a while with you. Take time for solitude, relaxation, for meditation to ease your pain (see p. 23). To the extent that you are able to, give the gifts of love, understanding and caring to yourself and to one another.

Perhaps you are going away for the holidays. Some families find it easier to go somewhere new to avoid painful associations, whilst others derive great comfort from returning to scenes of former happiness. There are those who find it difficult to leave the security of home for quite a time after a death. Take one another's needs into account when making plans. Sometimes compromises may have to be arrived at. The return home after the first time away can be very painful initially, as you re-enter the atmosphere of loss. Being forewarned eases the shock of return.

If this is the first holiday since your child died his/her siblings may feel their loss even more acutely than when distracted by school or their normal daily routine. You may be grieving too deeply to notice their needs – whether for understanding, help with scary emotions, playmates . . . Ask an appropriate person to take care whilst you are unable to.

The festive season is filled with symbolism. It is Christ's death that makes His birth a time for such rejoicing. Cycles continue, for death is never the end. Maybe you will light candles this holiday in memory of your child and to encourage your surviving children; for light dispels darkness. Faith and happiness can be rekindled and will in time take on new dimensions.

4. Birthdates, anniversaries: "How can we demonstrate our love?"

Does this question seem a strange one, unexpected in relation to dates now associated with pain and longing?

So many people after the death of a child can think only of their loss. A date of birth or of death approaches and they are filled with dread, panic and confusion. They ask: "How do I get through the day?"

"Will I feel as awful as I did last year?" "Will anyone remember?" "What if my other children ignore the anniversary?" "What if, on their sib's birthdate, they want a party – what do I do?" "And if my teenagers refuse to visit the cemetery with me, what then?"

Let us come back to the question: "How can we demonstrate our love?" Perhaps it is the clue we need, the source of an appropriate response. There is a difference between expressing devotion and perpetrating grief. I have no doubt that much pain is experienced in relation to the dates of birth and death of a cherished child, yet how best can you express the love you hold for him/her and for your surviving children? This could be the key issue in finding a satisfying solution for all the questions asked.

Each person will have ideas of his own. Sharing thoughts and feelings helps smooth out dissension, for understanding leads to mutually acceptable decisions. There are so many ways to show love and it is both gratifying and comforting to find answers to creative questions. The moment that affirmation becomes the central issue, the pain of loss becomes secondary. Instead of "How will I/we manage?" the focus becomes "What can I/we do for you, in your name?"

The fact that you grieve signifies that in your life there has been a person worth celebrating. Give great thanks for that precious life that has been lived, even though its span has been all too short. Find ways of meaningfully commemorating your child: e.g. plant a tree, fill your garden with flowering plants, give to someone in need, to a charity, or start a fund in his/her name. Make an offering to your church, synagogue, school or hospital . . . the list of possibilities is endless.

Plan the birthdate or anniversary activity that will appropriately express your love as a family. If you are on your own ask someone you care about to participate with you in the planning and the day. Pool your thoughts, needs and memories and share in the healing that you can allow to take place. You have choices. To what meaningfully creative conclusions can you come?

5. How long alive; how long dead?

Bereaved parents tell me that they experience an emptiness when they realise that their child has been longer dead than alive. Thoughts rush into that vacuum: this is unreal, unnatural. I am a forgotten parent in terms of my validity and role regarding that child. I feel displaced and scared: who will remember him/her?

I believe the Nigerians speak of *sasa* and *zamani* in relation to their dead. *Sasa* is the afterlife in which the deceased resides until there is no longer a single living person left who remembers or has heard of him. With the passing of that last one the deceased moves into *zamani*, or oblivion. This view illustrates parental sensitivity to a child's relevance in his/her community and to how quickly s/he might be forgotten.

For parents whose very young child has died these concerns may be the more acute: there has been little chance for a small child to have made a mark in society, and the parents are still relatively raw from their loss. (If a child has only lived for a year, in a brief twelve months they already face this "equator anniversary".)

Parents whose older children died have more time in which to heal before being faced with this issue, yet may have a greater sense of shock precisely because so much time has passed. But is there not also a victory in having coped and come through, however little or much time has gone by?

Human memory is frail and short; spiritual significance, whatever form it takes, is eternal – perhaps that puts the whole issue in a different and a more comforting light.

The realisation that a son or daughter has been gone for longer than the time spent with you here can, without guilt or disloyalty, herald the beginning of a new phase.

6. The "equator experience"

"Later this month," my friend said to me, "my little son will have been dead longer than he was alive."

"How do you feel about that?" I asked.

"I feel that he is moving away from me, that he's less and less mine . . ." She has now spent the span of his lifetime without him.

How mysterious existence is. How disturbing the sense of a widening gulf as time, and we with it, go on whilst a child who died seems to us to be fixed, caught in the past. We see a short life as an island receding, as increasingly the ocean of absence widens and extends and separates us from it.

"Did it all happen or was he just a dream, an illusion?" The present reality of pain has weight and texture: the past at times seems flimsy. The parenting heart cries out: "No, he was mine, ours, he was real, so loved and special." And asks, "Where is he now? Longer dead than alive, and for us the only reality is here."

My friend said: "In a way it's a new beginning for me. I can make a fresh start, be positive in outlook." And I felt her add, "and yet, and yet . . ."

Psychologically, intellectually, define it as you will, we can only deal with reality. Illusion is beyond us. But do we know the true dimensions of reality?

Let me tell you a story: Once upon a time not long ago a beautiful woman called Margaret was awaiting the birth of her first child. Her husband, Daniel, shared in the joy of her pregnancy, the wonder of growth, the expectancy of parenthood.

Now Daniel had the gift of "sight". He was able to perceive reality as it manifests, beyond the everyday perception of most men and women. And so he knew that this child was to share a part of life with them, not to be possessed, but as a fellow traveller.

Margaret bore this child knowing only that she had felt him quicken in her womb and, watching her body extend, that she not only carried the child but was also filled with welcome. The labour, though painful and long, was one of love. They named him Joseph and he grew from a delightful infant into a mischievous young child.

One day, when Joseph was four years old, he grew sick and died. Margaret, in her confusion, pain and despair, was beside herself with grief and anger that her beautiful son was dead. Daniel, with an anguished heart, wept bitter tears at their loss, both for Margaret in her distress and for himself in his terrible loneliness. Yet Daniel could see that Joseph, though physically gone from their presence, was healed, was alive and well and returning to his timeless origin.

Joseph's parents bore their grief, experiencing all the feelings of submergence and surfacing that human beings endure. For Daniel there was none of Margaret's need to make contact with their son to reassure herself that he was alright, to receive some sign . . . He did not have to search. He had tried to tell her what he knew but she would not hear. "You are crazy!" she would cry, "I bore him and if I have lost touch with him and see him no more, what you have to say can bring me no comfort." Margaret scorned Daniel's words and believed only in her limited idea of reality. As a result her grief was more acute and her sense of hopelessness the greater.

Four years passed and one day Daniel came upon Margaret packing all of Joseph's clothes and toys. Until then she had been unable to part with even one of them. Daniel approached her with great tenderness and asked her to explain. She replied, "Joseph has been gone now for as long a time as he was here with us. It is a sort of 'equator experience' – there is as much above, in a sense, as there is below. It seems as if this relates not only to time, but to life as well. I have to believe that such a gift from God as he was will not be destroyed. Indeed I think I recognise now that the light that is Joseph burns on, and so I do not need to keep his things any longer. There is in me, at last, a realisation that 'goodbye' is really only a bidding one another 'fare well'. That must mean that we move on and should leave the past where it belongs."

Daniel held Margaret close for a long time and they were filled with thankfulness and peace, and felt the quickening of a new beginning.

7. "No, he does not live (here) anymore"

Parents speak about how upsetting it is and how unprepared they always are for the shock of some communication through the post or by telephone addressed to their deceased child (e.g. a notification that he is to report for an army camp) or concerning him/her (e.g. "Re the Estate of the Late . . .", or "We notice that your account has not been used for some time . . ."). There are scores of instances and many of them are communications sent in spite of the relevant parties having been informed, sometimes repeatedly, that your child died. So often they arrive when the family members still need to avoid such confrontations.

There do not seem to be any simple ways of preventing such occurrences (and of course where estates are concerned they must be wound up).

● **Some practical ways of coping with these problems**
☐ Recognise that occasionally a letter or a call that will be upsetting will come. To some extent "forewarned is forearmed" and if you can say to yourself as the shockwave hits you, "Here it is; I knew it had to come", you may find it a little easier – and perhaps still easier the next time.

☐ If your response is an emotional one, express it. Release the feelings of anger or grief. Shout aloud or in your head, pound the table or a pillow, cry, tell someone how you are feeling or write it all down. Get rid of as much of the tension as you can.

☐ If your reaction is one of cold withdrawal I would encourage you to seek help in dealing with it. Healing cannot take place if you are repressing emotions. I do not suggest that withdrawal is necessarily pathological: some people, more usually men, find expression of feelings very threatening. But shutting them away is storing them, and this is not a safe thing to do. The stockpile mounts, requires a huge expenditure of energy to keep under control and becomes more difficult to handle as it gathers momentum.

☐ A retaliatory or punitive reaction is a danger signal too, because in this case acting on it can have undesirable results. Your feelings may be running so high that you do not care what happens except that "somebody has to get it". Count to ten a number of times; this sounds facile but if it interrupts the thrust of a fist in a face, it is worthwhile. If you can retaliate indirectly, e.g. write a scorching letter and then burn it, you will be far better off for having released feelings without laying yourself open to counter-attack.

☐ Ahead of time, plan ways of helping yourself and each other through the situations that set you back. I have made a number of basic suggestions. Your own solutions will work best for you. The important thing is to be prepared and take appropriate action so that you are not left feeling helpless and distraught when the situations arise.

8. Inquests, hearings

When my seventeen year old daughter was knocked down by a hit-and-run motorist, she spent two weeks in the Intensive Care Unit at the Johannesburg General Hospital, hovering between life and death. The driver, when traced, refused to take any responsibility whatsoever. My anger, desire for revenge and a choking sense of impotence knew no bounds. I experienced the frightening destructiveness of such wild rage that I was terrified that I might meet this man at the hospital. (The sisters told me he was constantly enquiring as to whether or not she had died.) I was not sure that I would not tear him apart. The intensity of emotion and my helplessness almost tore me apart. I knew I would be very ill if I did not let go of my rage, but I had no idea what to do about it. I distracted myself and avoided the issue as best I could.

There are times when circumstances seem to challenge all that is finest within us if we wish to come through with our integrity intact.

Inquests, press reports, court hearings (sometimes in relation to medical queries) are further examples of this sort of challenge; a testing of our spiritual and emotional maturity and of what standards we choose to live by.

So often an inquest or hearing seems to by-pass what we consider to be just: witnesses are not called, or a sentence is passed that appears to make a mockery of the sanctity of human life. Sometimes press reports are written without accuracy or sensitivity and cause further anger, pain and confusion. Of course it is not always like this, but families do anticipate with trepidation and fear the re-opening of wounds.

If you are faced with (or have been through) such challenges and are having difficulty, there is some inner work that can be done in your attitude towards them. I refer here to an *in-quest*, a personal search within for compassion and forgiveness; your own *hearing* of true values. This is the way in which I was eventually able to relinquish my anger and vengefulness.

I am approaching this from the viewpoint that we are here on earth to learn, teach, restore balance and amend old wrongs; that we develop integrity and spiritual refinement if we use circumstances as opportunities for growth. Bearing negativity and destructiveness benefits no-one. Whilst you might feel that wrongdoing must be paid for, the re-occurrence of negligence (or whatever the issue) be prevented, and that as a parent you owe it to your child to see justice done, these are matters that can only be successfully dealt with when you are not in the grip of your emotions. If your attitude is negative you arouse negativity; if possible, you invite constructive results. This is the practicality of the truly spiritual response.

If we expect forgiveness, how can we offer others anything less? The truly loving person says, "This is the good I want for you because I value myself." If Christ could pray on the cross, "Forgive them, for they know not what they do", with the finest compassion for those crucifying Him, should we, if we are to express the godliness that is within us, not endeavour to offer no less?

In dealing with your anger and distress there is a profoundly important choice for you to make that affects not only your peace and well-being but that of others as well. The ripples of compassion and forgiveness go out and out . . . and return again. In the fullness of time all are held responsible for their errors and the consequences will have to be faced. Thus though justice may not seem to have been meted out we may trust that in time the balance will be restored.

How to cope . . .

C With relationships and loss

1. Marriage and loss

Marriage unites; grief places the emphasis on individuality. Each person has his/her own style and rhythm of grieving which, according to personality, temperament and past experiences of loss will form their own pattern. Rarely will both marital partners be "in step" with one another's mourning. Mutual support during times of stress may always have been taken for granted, but, as Sarnoff-Schiff (1979:58) observes: ". . . you cannot lean on something bent double from its own burden". Thus each of you must, to some extent, cope on your own without much help from your mate. If this is not understood, unmet expectations can lead to angry disappointment, a sense of rejection or even abandonment, so high do feelings run after the death of a child. They generally remain unresolved because constructive communication does not come easily when you are deeply distressed.

In another common situation, one spouse (usually the husband) sets his needs aside, postpones or blocks his own grieving so as to remain available as the protector and comforter. When his wife is over the worst, he finds himself in dire need of patience and empathy so that he may come to terms with his pain. But by now it is expected that he, too, has mourned and is able to relinquish his grief.

When one or both partners block their emotions because they fear being overwhelmed by their pain, they find themselves in the same predicament. When ready to begin dealing with it no-one is paying them attention anymore; indeed it is assumed that they are "over it". They are looked at askance when signs of grief emerge. This is a difficult and unhealthy situation.

If you are caught between distress and expectations, and do not feel you have the right to ask those around you to listen and support you, find a counsellor or therapist. Grief does not just dissolve; it must be worked through.

When both of you are actively mourning you will generally find, because individual rhythms are different, that one of you is having an

66

easier day whilst the other is immersed in suffering. The partner who has surfaced for a while, with head above water, so to say, is naturally reluctant to submerge again to assist the other – and this is where the dissonance spoken of earlier, comes in.

What can be done? Whenever possible, express mutual love, respect and caring, whether verbally or non-verbally. Bear in mind the individuality of response to loss, and try to be patient and understanding with each other.

In grief, as at any other time in life, there is a choice of attitude that must consciously be taken. The gist of it is as follows: Are you going to allow yourself to be destroyed by pain and despair, or will you hold as steady as possible whilst working at resolving your anguish, trusting that in time all will be well? There is value in expressing courage; it is one way of making it yours.

Try calling problems "opportunities" from now on. You will find that the emphasis changes, becoming far more creative.

Do not sweep difficulties under the carpet: it is bad marriage-keeping. Air and clear them as far as possible. Deal with issues related or unrelated to the death. Refusal to do so is indicative of great anger, and that must be acknowledged and resolved. (There is a section on anger on p. 42.)

Not allowing emotions to build up to a pitch but defusing them as they gather momentum is wise – and far easier on all concerned. The practice of on-going communication is the key.

Differences of opinion, whether they have been about care of the child pre-death, concerning funeral arrangements, how best to manage family affairs now . . . must be relinquished. If not they may fester, and such wounds do not heal successfully. Let go of blame: you have lost enough without allowing your marriage to be at risk too. Indeed, accusation even just harboured in the mind drives a wedge between people. If your marriage is to survive and have meaning, deal in a creative way with any reproaches or condemnation that lie between you. If not, hurts are piled upon hurt, and in time afflict your relationship. Talk it through if you can do so safely. Otherwise get assistance to resolve the issues.

Be aware, if you find the sharing of emotions very stressful, that ongoing silence can erect barriers. The solution for both the communicator and the one who has withdrawn, is in being prepared to listen. Often it is by being attentive that you begin to perceive, even in the absence of words, how your mate is feeling. (Turning to crutches

67

such as nicotine, liquor, or drugs is the subject of p. 20: you may want to read it if you tend to rely on any of them.)

Do not plan major changes in your lives during the first year after a death unless forced by circumstances to do so. Later on you may perceive them to have been rash decisions. If financial insecurity is a strain on you at present, ask for advice or perspective from your bank manager or a trusted advisor. Whilst mourning, your reasoning is not as clear and objective as you might think.

Seeking extra-marital comfort may be a temptation, yet it generates great inner discomfort. Vulnerable as you both are at present, you are ill-equipped to cope with any additional strain. Rather find the solution to the need for consolation in sharing and mutual understanding. For bereaved parents the question of physical intimacy is often a difficult one because individuals respond so differently to their circumstances. One of you may be yearning for the solace that sexual closeness provides whilst the other inwardly screams, "How *can* you be thinking of sex when our child is gone?"

How do you see the sexual act at the moment? A comfort, renewal, an escape, your due, the origin of the child now dead? Does it signify the risk of an, at present, unthinkable pregnancy? Is withholding yourself from you partner an act of defiance due to anger? Talk about your feelings and endeavour to resolve any impasse. Be patient, try to be caring, prepared to compromise. Do not demand too much of one another. Be aware that exhaustion, so very common in the bereaved, plays a part here too. Seek help if communication is not possible or fruitful. It can be a great relief to talk to a responsible, objective outsider.

Sexuality, by the way, is the life principle: in the face of death it affirms the viable. It is in essence a giving, rather than a getting. When two people agree to be close and comfort one another their relationship is deepened and the marriage taken to new, enriching levels.

It is important to realise that having enjoyment is not disloyal to your deceased child. Recovery must take place if the loss is not to be compounded. No son or daughter would wish his/her parent to grieve endlessly. It is therefore your right, in your child's name, to facilitate your healing in every way possible.

Religious/spiritual conflict or despair might arise between marriage partners after the death of a child. Many mourners base rejection and anger towards God on the assumption that He has snatched their child from them – and they ask why, and what sort of God can do such an appalling thing? These questions, unattended, generate huge anger, remorse and fear. They are issues central to healing. It is wise to speak to your minister about them. (You will find a relevant section on p. 53.)

Mention must be made of the constructive aspects of a mutual loss: You and your spouse together gave life and love to your child. You are united through the beauty of your memories and the intimacy of wordless understanding. There may be respect for and increased knowledge of each other as you ride the storm of grief. The shared experience of so profound a loss can be binding. Greater closeness often follows insight and new-found strengths.

It has been said that people are like trees: they perceive their branches, leaves and flowering. But it is their pain that takes them down into their root-system to yield self-knowledge that would not have been otherwise attained. And are the roots of trees not intertwined in the ground of their being?

2. The step-parent and bereavement

The categories I divide this subject into are:
- ☐ The *new* step-parent, who has been a family member for up to one year
- ☐ The *well-established* step-parent, who has been in this role for many years
- ☐ The *post-event* step-parent, who has joined the family after the death of a child.

Whichever of the three categories you are in, as a step-parent you may have the problem that some people do not recognize or acknowledge your grief. You may find yourself constantly by-passed in their concern for the natural parents' welfare. (Siblings also often have this difficult situation to deal with when everyone expresses distress about their parents' pain and ignores theirs.) It is confusing and can generate a great deal of anger to be left feeling an outsider to the family. You might wish to state quite clearly that the family's pain is your own. However you wish to respond, you do not have to bear malice for often people know not what they do.

● *The new step-parent*
Whether or not you have known the deceased child for many years

69

prior to your marriage to his/her mother or father, you have only been in an active parenting role for a short time. You may or may not have been accepted by your spouse and step-child(ren) as influential in their lives. The particular dynamics of your marriage, of the family, and the ages of the children are relevant in terms of the position you find yourself in after the death of your step-son/daughter. Because so many factors are specific to each family's unique circumstances, I will have to generalise here about the new step-parent's situation.

☐ *The most common difficulties that confront you:*
   ☐ You might feel that though you grieve over the death of the child you have little right to do so, for you have known him/her for so short a time.
   ☐ Your spouse may challenge you, saying that you cannot possibly understand his/her feelings and can therefore be of little comfort. This predicament can pose a threat to your marriage, an added worry.

A fair amount of inner security and a great deal of patience are helpful in weathering these storms. It is important not to take the natural parent's words too personally. Challenges and accusations are responses to pain, and sometimes it is better that they are verbalized rather than repressed. What is not given expression to is stored and tends to emerge later, the accumulation compounding the feelings that trigger the eventual release.

☐ *Guidelines to cope with these problems*
   ☐ Try not to take offence.
   ☐ Allow your spouse to off-load emotions, but do not be afraid to set limits upon any extremes of expression (yours or his/hers), whether in terms of duration or of intensity; e.g. violence – verbal or physical.
   ☐ If your spouse excludes you, refusing to share thoughts and feelings
      a. offer your love and support;
      b. communicate as best you can the value of maintaining your relationship during the mourning period;
      c. exercise great patience.

☐ Find someone with whom you can share your grief and concerns so that you have support and understanding.

☐ Perhaps you might want to suggest counselling to assist your spouse, yourself, the whole family.

In their grief, your remaining step-children may be turning to you for help and guidance, or rejecting both you and your role. Feelings are intense during bereavement. Set limits that you think are reasonable, and be forebearing. It you feel unsure as to how to cope, consult someone who can explain the dynamics of grief and be your guide.

You have a right to your sorrow. It is hard to have that denied you. But if, on the other hand, you are not grieving accept it without a sense of guilt. Feelings cannot be "made to order" and there is always a good subjective reason for them. Being inwardly honest and accepting yourself will make you feel more secure and of greater value to the family. When normal living patterns are restored, they may understand your feelings and then new relationships can be built.

● *The well-established step-parent*
The level of interaction and acceptance within your family will have a great deal to do with whether or not you are in an in-step-parent or an out-of-step-parent after the death of one of the children.

Any marriage is under strain when a child dies, and the health and strength of the relationship is truly tested. Perhaps you think you are grieving as deeply as your spouse, or maybe that in your particular situation you cannot be. Much of what has been said in the section above applies to you as well. The main difference is that because your role as step-parent is not new there may be fewer unexpected reactions as waves of grief hit the family.

If you have had difficulty in being accepted by all the members of the family, you will probably find that the situation will worsen under stress. Yet loss has been known to bring people together when there is understanding, compassion and a strong desire to keep the unit from suffering any further trauma.

If you are feeling excluded by the family during this difficult time, communication is a key to resolving the problem. If you can talk it through together, so much the better; if not, find someone who can help you gain perspective. Generally speaking, leaving important issues alone in the hope that they will resolve themselves is not very successful.

Remember, grief is a process and goes through many changing phases. Family members will not be keeping in step with one another.

You are entitled to your emotions; indeed to be a parent, with a parent's feelings, you do not have to have physically given form to that child.

● *The post-event step-parent*

You have married a grieving parent and perhaps there are unresolved feelings complicating your relationship. You may or may not have ever known the child who died. If not, you are largely unable to share in an area of your wife/husband's life that is particularly important and thought-consuming at present. Maybe you are able to bring great comfort.

If your relationship with your spouse and/or step-children is under a lot of strain, encourage your partner to have grief-counselling, or perhaps marriage guidance or family therapy. The child that resides within every person, whatever their age, tends to emerge in stressful situations and needs to be appropriately dealt with for resoluiton of grief. This generally means a necessity for comfort, holding, reassurance, understanding and sometimes limit-setting.

Whatever your reasons were for marrying, examine them again. If they still hold good, have patience and keep an awareness of both them and your marriage vows. Should they seem to have been ill-founded, can you both redefine them in a mutually affirming way? Come to no hasty decisions; perspective is lost during the time of mourning and it takes time, common sense and goodwill to regain it.

● *Problematic issues relevant to all bereaved step-parents*

By marrying your present partner you have, in a sense, taken the place of your deceased step-child's one parent. There may be difficulties relating to the double loss for (whether the previous spouse died or divorced) a separation took place. Even in a family which has felt relief at the ending of a relationship there has been a deprivation of one sort or another. A death is linked by association with other losses and thus the present grief is complicated because family members are dealing with varying emotional responses. Some of these may come as a shock if unexpected. Your spouse may have thought that the feelings related to the death or divorce of his/her first marriage partner had been re-solved, but finds now that there are painful issues that re-emerge. You may need counselling to help sort out and make sense of all that is going on. When the reasons behind responses which seem irrational are understood, they become a lot simpler to deal with.

If your wife/husband was widowed/widowered, the death of the child could be seen to be bringing about a reunion between the two deceased family members. Because the bereaved yearn for their loved ones and often wish to join them, you may be excluded and feel almost irrelevant. Great tolerance and understanding will be required until your spouse is again able to recognise the worth of living with present relationships. Perhaps you can help her/him to find comfort in the child's being taken care of by the other parent. Often the bereaved want reassurance that their childen are alright.

When the previous marriage was ended by divorce and a child died, grief can make a relationship with the parent who left, pertinent once more. The shared parenting and love for that child constitute a bond that may be validated by the mutual sense of loss. If that parent returns, the children in the family are likely to become confused. At best their loyalties will be divided (a most difficult situation for them to cope with) and at worst you may be rejected for a while. Nevertheless, you may have to allow your spouse time with his/her former mate.

Every family is unique, and it is impossible to generalise beyond saying that such situations require sensitivity and tact and that they generally can be resolved. Because there are so many concurrent problems it is exceedingly difficult for anyone who is subjectively involved to have sufficient perspective and be unemotional enough to sort them all out. It is wise, therefore, to seek professional help.

3. The single parent and loss

If you are carrying on and trying to do the best you can as a bereaved and single parent, you are a special person indeed! There are certain difficulties that you face (alone) that are specific to your situation. Some discussion of a number of them may be helpful to you.

The fact that you are a single parent may be due to free choice with no grief involved, or to bereavement, separation or divorce. A death always evokes in the mourner the feelings associated with any previous significant loss. Thus, if you have been through the mill, you are probably finding that you are now having to deal with the residues of the grief that you experienced prior to the death of your child, in addition to your present pain. (When my father died twelve years after my mother's death I found I was mourning both of them; I kept recalling all that my mother had meant to me as I wept for my father. A painful separation or divorce can have the same effect). Be gentle with yourself; you have a great deal to cope with. Grieving takes time and consistent work.

When a child dies, both father and mother find themselves so bowed down with bereftness that they are unable to support each other for quite some time. Thus although you do not have the partnering-parent of your child with you, you are not necessarily more alone with your pain than a married person. Any parent needs to find someone to whom s/he can express the overwhelming feelings experienced. Because family members usually protect one another, that confidante is often a person outside the immediate family circle. If you are not already doing so, share your grief with whoever you think will be able to understand.

Perhaps your child's death has brought your ex-mate back into your life and this is proving difficult for you. Is grief being used as an excuse to re-establish the connection? You will have to gain clarity and decide what is best under the circumstances. If you feel compromised, say so. The reason for breaking your relationship is unlikely to be changed for the better by the loss of your child.

If your son's/daughter's death has brought you and your mate together again and that is what you both want, do not feel guilty about any happiness you may be experiencing; see it as a gift your child could give you. You may think how sad it is that it had to be in this way, but you will work through that grief. Give yourself time.

As a single parent your distress may relate to feelings of compassion for your child's other parent, without your having the freedom to be of any comfort. Knowing that another is suffering without being able to offer help, is very hard. If you cannot meet, telephone, cable or write, surround him/her with the thoughts you want to convey. Think deeply about this. A great deal can travel along the lines of interpersonal bonds.

Bereavement brings with it a sense of insecurity and inadequacy. Being single, you may be particularly vulnerable to these feelings. As a grieving bread-winner you might feel tense and worried if you are unable to concentrate, have become forgetful and think you cannot manage your job. These are all normal signs of mourning, but very disturbing when you feel that so much depends on your ability to cope. It is frightening to wonder whether you can deal with your surviving children's needs on your own, or with your loneliness if you have no dependants.

A grieving parent is too emotionally taxed to manage really competently with the children's grief – indeed with anything more than basic daily requirements.

Compensation is likely to be a worry at present. Before your child's death you may have been feeling that you have to make up to your children for the lack of a father/mother in the home. Now you have another loss to compensate for. How difficult that must be, believing you are obliged to recompense your family for all that is missing. It cannot be done, and there might be a sense of remorse behind your need. If so, it does not help to see the situation as being your fault; nor will anything be resolved by placing unrealistic expectations upon yourself. It is in facing circumstances together that a family's coping skills are developed. The situation you and your dependants find yourselves in provides you all with opportunities for step-by-step learning, as a team, each at his/her own level. Such victories of growth build self-assurance and strength.

So rather turn your attention to providing what you can to the best of your ability, and when necessary ask suitable others to fill the gap. We are members of a community and, when appropriate, should be willing to offer to and receive from those around us.

Guilt is a monster that stalks all but the impervious. (See p. 45.) I will only refer here to blame and self-blame in the context of the single parent. Perhaps you are condemning yourself for your child's death. Is this realistic or unrealistic? Share your feelings with someone who can give you perspective and help you through this nightmare.

Perhaps your ex-partner is blaming you, or you him/her. The accusations may be well-founded or totally unreasonable. Often there is great anger in grief. Once again, share this burden, whether you are the accuser or the accused. It may seem as if adequate repentance and forgiveness can never, nor should ever, be possible under these circumstances. There are many steps through anger and grief to be taken before penitence, forgiveness and the God-given grace to accept it is yours. Place this issue in His hands.

If mourning the absence of a loved partner, the loss of a child and/or suffering from extreme guilt, you may experience in you a strong desire to end your life. Life may appear to be without meaning at present. Perhaps it seems as if too much is being asked of you in your struggle alone. But you are reading this, and that indicates that there is some spark of desire to survive. Life itself is the reason to live. Many in similar circumstances have won through. It can be done, and you are not alone.

Understanding and reassurance are offered by The Compassionate Friends. In addition, counselling or psycho-therapy will provide you with professional help. Perhaps your minister is the right person to assist you. It is important that you recognise that you are so vulnerable at the moment that it is unwise to try to cope with your grief and suicidal thoughts on your own.

Take courage; help is available and your spirit has strength beyond your reckoning. Choose to heal: that is the first thing to do. You will come through this dark period by taking just one step at a time. That is all you need to know to give yourself the opportunity to discover that recovery is indeed worthwhile.

4. Death of an only child

I

Most of us desire and need to parent. It is far more than a natural biological urge based on preservation of the species. It is with our total being that we long to have children, and having borne them we become deeply involved with their care, protection and upbringing.

The death of a younster goes against the natural order of life. When it is an only child it may seem that there is nothing left to live for. Your son/daughter, of whatever age, is not physically here any longer, and with that bereavement the present and future seem meaningless.

You may be asking how you can endure and how to heal. Here are some questions and comments designed to direct your thoughts along helpful lines. They touch on you the individual, your marriage, and you as parent. Who you are and how you perceive these two roles have a great deal to do with your grief, your attitudes and recovery.

● *You, the individual*
What has been your focus prior to your loss? If your child was the centre of your world creative involvements now become essential; your life must include new interests if healing is to take place.

Have you had enthusiasm for hobbies or have you tended, on the whole, to concentrate your attention and energies on work? Has there been a balance between the many facets of your daily life? Prior interests are there to return to and new ones are for the making if you need them.

Have you had a healthy self-regard or tended to belittle yourself and feel inadequate and guilty? Recovery from grief can mean a fresh start: it is not only possible but wise to make the grief experience personally meaningful. As you work through it you wil be learning about recovery, about finding the positive, about your own abilities . . . Good can emerge from tragedy.

Has religion or a spiritual outlook played a significant part in your life? Perhaps you are an atheist or an agnostic. Whatever your orientation, there is a well-trodden path through mourning and you are not alone.

At first it does not seem as if there can ever be recovery, or that there is energy or sufficient resolve even to make a start. You are just hanging on and going through the motions of living. But the grief process is unfolding, and very gradually it gets a little easier to bear the sorrow. After a while some energy is available and it becomes possible to make a creative choice.

Whatever your style of being, you have been confronted with the challenge of dealing with your loss and rehabilitating yourself. You have to choose between sinking or swimming. It is remarkable to see parents recovering from the most unbelievable pain, given time and taking the decision to do so. Certainly the death of any child leaves family members anguished, whilst the loss of an only child carries its own specific demands. The choice to journey through and climb above the grief must be individually made.

● *Your marriage*
What was the state of your marriage before the death, and how is it faring now? Partnerships undergo an enormous amount of strain when a child dies. (See p. 66).

Marriages can be strengthened by the sharing of pain. Recognise that though there is great bereftness in your lives, all is not lost. Your union can emerge the stronger for the shared experience – even though very often you will find yourselves out of step with one another.

Maybe at the moment you are completely at odds: do not despair. Mourning is a series of phases each of which gives way to the next in due time. With real concern for your marriage, compassion for and patience with your spouse, all can be healed.

● *You, as parent*
Perhaps your relationship with your child was a close and fulfilling one. Maybe there was much friction and divergence of personalities.

You might be relatively free of self-condemnation, or struggling with it. If the latter, refer to p. 48.

Many parents, after the death of an only child, tend to idealise him/her; however, your child must be grieved as a real person. Seeing only the best sides means denying the others. This leads to anger because your pain does not abate, and no-one really recognises the ideal you project. It is wonderful to be human! The super-being has no challenges or victories, no times when s/he needs your comfort or help. Was your child really like that? Weaknesses and strengths are all acceptable and no judgement is necessary.

Perhaps you will have other children in the future. No child replaces the one who died, but another does help to fill the gap that has been left and becomes a source of real joy. Maybe it is not possible for you to bear more children. Yet, as I have already said, are we not, in a deep and extensive sense, parents to all youngsters? At present that seems cold comfort; you want your own son/daughter back. Of course you do. But I am thinking of a couple who lost their only child and now, some years later, are god-parents to a number of their friends' children. They are much comforted thereby. Whether or not you are a god-parent you can play a part in other boys' and girls' lives in appropriate and mutually fulfilling ways.

Do not become so absorbed by your grief that you lose your child in an even more profound sense. (See "Restoration" on p. 52.) Go beyond your anguish to remember your child with tenderness and appreciation. It is so easy during the dark days of pain to lose awareness of the light.

II

This section is not about your pain, and your suffering, but about some perspectives on the death of your only child that may be helpful.

My first question, "What have you lost?" relates to the physical presence of your son/daughter, with all that has meant to you.

My second question is, "What have you truly lost?" Careful consideration yields the realisation that it is not possible for you to no longer be a parent even though your child died. You have borne and/or parented and the value of that has been offered to the world. Good is never lost.

Parenting is more than a role: it is a state of being and cannot be cancelled out. You have not lost the essence of your child nor of the relationship with him/her. Life continues on other levels and physical separation does not alter that. The bonds between you hold.

My third question, "Who are you?", pertains to you in relation to your attitudes towards life, healing and growth, the living and the so-called dead. Have you been life-affirming (putting your energies creatively into living) prior to your loss and where is your focus now – on life or on death?

We are all parents to all children (yes, you are your brother's keeper), so in answer to "who are you?" you may be one who encompasses others. I recall Jesus' words to His mother before He died, "Woman, behold thy son" and to his disciple, "Behold thy mother". We do not only parent through blood ties. Choice of focus and of attitude towards life becomes increasingly yours as you progress through the grieving process. The death of your child puts the spotlight on who you choose to be or to become, because it is a time for change of outlook and priorities . . .

Your past has in part been made up of the privilege and joy of having a child. As you move on through life this remains behind and accompanies you. You remember and you are shaped thereby. Even as it is irretrievable so it is also part of any present moment. There is comfort to be drawn from that.

Your present may be filled with pain, but ever-present is the potential for healing, for surrounding yourself with people who are meaningful to you and for your giving to others. This potential signifies your ability to make what is possible a reality now.

Your future, though you may have no interest in it as present, is in God's and your hands. You constitute your own meanings: whilst life may seem to hold little of value, yet it rests with you what you will make of your situation and opportunities. Perhaps it is too soon to look ahead with anything but desolation and fearfulness; yet change is a constant in our lives. Do not forget that the dawn dispels the night.

5. Some thoughts on the death of an only son or daughter

At a deep level we all yearn for inner and outer completeness. A significant loss threatens our internal balance and disturbs the established family pattern – its structure and therefore its functioning as well. I discuss wholeness here because it is a relevant and a neglected subject with regard to this particular aspect of loss.

Relationships are indeed complex: you as father and as mother relate differently to your same-sex child than to the opposite-sex child, though both are likely to be equally precious to you. There is a natural balancing out: the gender identification between father and son, mother and daughter; and the complementarity of opposites, the father-daughter, mother-son interactions.

You may have lost your only son amidst girls or the one daughter in a family of boys. Perhaps your son or daughter has been long-awaited, his/her arrival even despaired of. Whether or not that is the case, that one "different" child has some special significance for your family.

● *A number of pertinent factors relating to the completeness referred to above*

☐ Role or gender-identification is natural and desirable. (This means your son taking his father as a model for his predominant masculinity, your daughter identifying with her mother for her predominantly feminine mode.) It establishes common ground: an often deep identification between you (the same-sex parent and child), like-interests, friendship, companionship. It is a basis for the delight found in relating to the opposite-sex child. Thus for both of you the death of an only son or daughter is likely to be a central loss.

☐ Each person is unique, special and loved for his/her personality, temperament, individuality, etc. regardless of gender. Yet there is a difference between a family which loses an only son or daughter and one in which there are other surviving boys or girls. There is usually a particular loneliness, however beloved the remaining children are.

☐ It is important to recognise how inadequate and perhaps non-special your surviving children may feel, knowing that they are not able to be a son if they are girls or a daughter if they are boys. In addition to their grief at the death of their sibling they carry "gender-guilt". They need you to confront this issue with honesty, whilst reassuring them of your love for and appreciation of them exactly as they are. Allow them to console you; children of any age and sex need to know they can be of comfort to their parents.

☐ Though your family is now incomplete it may help to remember that every individual carries both male and female aspects within his/her personality. If each member of your family develops and is/becomes comfortable with these two sides of inner being, even though one is dominant you will all be achieving a balance, a personal completeness in a different but most rewarding way. Companionship between family members will increase.

How effective to be able at times to relate to your spouse and children in matched masculine modes of efficiency, logic, drive, etc. and feminine modes of creativity, imaginativeness, nurture, intuition, etc. The complementary balancing of male and female aspects brings equilibrium, stability – and adds spice to your relationships.

So, deeply though you grieve your special loss, there are healing compensations within reach when you feel ready to find comfort and newness through them. What a beautiful way in which to honour and maintain the qualities of your child who died.

6. When a middle child has died

Bereaved parents often ask me what they should say to someone who, not knowing that there has been a death in the family, comments on the age gap between the surviving children: "My goodness, Lara is ten and Jason only four . . . why such a big difference?"

There is a void far more deeply felt than any casual acquaintance can imagine. As mourners you have your grief compounded by the realisation that a connecting link between your surviving children has gone, leaving a sharply felt loneliness and a new adjustment to be made in the eldest and youngest siblings' relationship.

What can you say? The decision is made in terms of who is asking. If it is someone with whom you will probably have no more interaction, you can say whatever seems the easiest. But if it is likely that you will have further contact then tell him/her you have lost a child. If you feel willing to talk about it, give that reassurance. If you do not, you can say so.

Some parents say that they feel they deny the existence of the deceased child by not mentioning him/her and they feel disloyal. If that is the case then s/he must be acknowledged.

It is difficult, particularly when unexpected, to cope with confrontations concerning loss. Does it not get a little easier each time you have to do so? That will depend upon factors such as the way you are feeling when the question is asked, but generally speaking the problems that bereaved parents and siblings encounter do lose their potency when dealt with repeatedly.

The changed relationship between your remaining children (who are now literally "next of kin") provides an opportunity to relate to one another in new ways not previously open to them. No doubt you would prefer things the way they were; but there *are* changes and it will help if they are worked with positively. Perhaps this seems disloyal to the child who died as if s/he is excluded by the closing of ranks. Yet the structure of the family has altered and so must its behaviour if healing is to take place. It does not mean that the absent one is forgotten or has no more relevance. S/he is present within and among you all. It will help you to adjust if you open yourselves to the creative possibilities that do exist.

In a sense Lara and Jason have known each other through their middle sibling. They now not only share grief but have a direct connection with each other. There is no longer a threeway interaction or two "camps" with one of them closer to the third child and the other left out. This is a challenge: life is precious and these two children have each other. Lara and Jason may draw close quite naturally or may need encouragement to do so. Even if their personalities are completely different, in their lonely sadness there is potential for sister- and brotherhood. They can discover each other anew.

If your eldest and youngest children were always close and the middle child was the one left out, his/her death will engender a sense of guilt in the others and they will need some help to resolve it. I suggest that they talk about their feelings and share their thoughts with whoever can help them most. Understanding and self-forgiveness will enable them to feel closer to their deceased sib and free them to mourn in a healthier way.

7. Loss of a child who was gay

Whatever the cause of death you may be having mixed feelings towards your gay daughter/son now that s/he is dead. See the chapter on homosexuality, AIDS and bereavement on p. 110). Read that in conjunction with this section.

I focus here on the unresolved, unhappy alliance between parent and child for those who are struggling to cope.

Maybe uppermost in your mind is the hollowness of your grief – the regrets in relation to what would have been "if things had only been different". You may have a great deal of anger towards this child, directed at yourself or against your spouse for his/her role in relation to the homosexuality.

After a death, alienation is either pushed away and not dealt with, or acknowledged:

☐ When alienation is *denied* (sometimes owing to shame), no effective solution can be found. Grief cannot be worked through to completion because one aspect of it is blocked.
☐ If *acknowledged*, there is a choice between
   ☐ holding on to the separateness and
   ☐ being prepared to deal with it and let it dissolve.

It is only then that the hollowness can be filled with your child's essence which has little if anything to do with his/her behaviour patterns. Your child's goodness is then being restored to you . . .

How tragic when disapproval drives a wedge between family members. If you have not been able to cope creatively with your son or daughter's homosexuality before his/her death, here is another opportunity to do so.

Think about your child; write down his/her good points. What made you happy, proud? In what ways did s/he please you? In what ways did s/he pleasantly surprise you? What potential did you see? Spend some time bringing to mind everything positive in your view of your child. I am not suggesting that you deny the negatives – all facets must be mourned – but get in touch with who s/he was in truth.

Having done so, can you see that someone valuable is emerging from your recollections? It is painful to mourn one you love, but how much more painful to think there is no-one lovable there to be mourned.

8. The death of a twin

Everything said about grief at the loss of a child applies when that child is a twin. I focus here specifically on the factors that relate to the significance of twinship and the death of one of the pair.

● *The parents' loss*
When a baby is expected many preparations and adjustments must be made. In some families there is excited anticipation and in others regrets and perhaps anxiety. When it becomes evident that not one but two infants are on the way, the emotions felt are intensified and adjustments have to be greater. There is often a sense of pride, of marked achievement: "We're going to have *twins!*"

If at birth the babies are identical there is usually closer attention paid them by family and friends, both so as to be able to tell them apart and due to fascination with their likeness. Greater notice is taken of you, the parents, by relatives, friends and even strangers – whether the twins are identical or not.

If their arrival has meant greater hardship, perhaps financial strain, the struggle brings with it mixed feelings that are natural and understandable.

If one of the twins dies in infancy the disappointment and grief in most cases are acute. You may reproach yourself that having one surviving babe is not a greater comfort to you than it is. Each child, being an individual, is mourned for him/herself and a whole shift has to take place again – from twins to one baby.

The adjustment from expecting one to two was made with delight or trepidation; the way back is filled with regrets and the loss of special plans. All the practical arrangements (two of everything and a special pram) serve as painful reminders of the death.

Perhaps, like some parents, you are suffering self-condemnation because you did not feel a greater sense of welcome. Carried to extremes you may even feel responsible for the death because having to provide for twins was such a burden. The loss may seem to be a punishment. Thoughts and feelings did not cause the death: this is unrealistic thinking. Talk it through with someone who can help you to relinquish it and gain perspective.

Between most twins, whether or not they get on well together, there is a special connection which I believe has much to do with their shared experience in utero. You may be recognising this, even if not consciously, and so, in addition to the grief over the death of your son/daughter, you might be disturbed about the deep significance of that separation to the remaining twin, and not know what to do to help him/her.

Complicating matters further is the fact that this child is a poignant and constant reminder of the loss. Such mixed feelings churn within: "Thank heaven we have the one twin left . . . I cannot bear to see his/her loneliness now . . . s/he is a painful reminder – I cannot bear it . . ." and so on.

Those who have suffered the terrible experience of losing both children will admonish those with a single bereavement to count their blessings and treasure whoever is left. But the mixed and changeable thoughts and emotions naturally do ebb and flow.

To consider the death of an identical twin is to go deeper into the difficult dynamics that twinship presents. For the most part I address this issue in the next section (re the loss to the twin). But because you and your family, due to their physical alikeness, are visually constantly confronted by each/both of the twins after the death of the one, I must deal with it here as well.

The focus on loss being so dominant in grief, the presence of the deceased child's face and form is likely for some time to be a sharp and agonizing reminder rather than a comfort. It might arouse conflicting and confusing feelings about the surviving twin. But you have not lost both children and so the remaining one needs reassurance that s/he can be of comfort. Both you and s/he know how hard it is to bear the likeness. This is where sensitivity and honesty are so necessary: being blunt about your pain may wound and bring about desperation and possible withdrawal. If you can be caringly genuine with each other you will establish solid ground on which to proceed. Trust leads to further sharing, consolation and deepened relationships.

If the similarity of the twins causes you anguish, exploring the remaining child's individuality as a separate person can help. This twin must go on to develop in his/her own way. You can assist in the enormous adjustment s/he has to make by perceiving him/her as a separate individual. Whatever you are able to do to support and aid your children will comfort you. So in having the courage to work at this new definition of independent identity, though painful because it emphasises the loss, you will move towards healing as well. If you have always recognised your twins' individuality this will be easier.

Perhaps your reaction is wanting to cling to your departed son/daughter, not feeling ready or willing to accept the separation of which I speak. Yet a changing situation is already in process. The attempt to hold on is natural, but grief is only resolved when you can let go.

● *The loss to the twin*

I am a bereaved twin, and so know the particular bonding that can exist. Let's look at *two categories of twins:*

☐ *Those with inner identification (whether identical or not):* A deep bond is experienced by closely relating twins, and like all other bonds of love, it is not severed by death. Mourning and pining are acute because the physical absence is felt so intensely. For some it is as if one half of themselves has gone – a sense of amputation – and that is a frightening ordeal to live with, even for a while. Talking about these feelings helps. In time their severity will lessen.

□ *Those who are separate beings from the outset:* The dynamics of this group are more akin to those of the death of a sibling – although the shared uterine experience still has some bearing. Perhaps the effects of twinship in this case are determined more by societal expectations and responses. (A sense of close kinship cannot be demanded and there should be no blame attached to anyone if your twins have not been close.)

It is quite likely that the surviving brother/sister will go through some self-accusation after the death and, if acute, will project it onto the deceased twin to relieve the inner tension. This can be problematic because it is hard to hear criticism of a child who has died. Nevertheless the remaining one needs your patience and understanding. (See coping with the grief of children in Part II.)

Survivor guilt is often more keenly felt by the remaining twin than by other siblings. Twins have shared conception, uterine environment, birth and many (if not most) life events. They may have been dressed alike and had the same toys. Now so momentous an event as death has come to one and not the other. "Why did you have to die and leave me?" and "I don't want to go on living without you" are two responses often heard. There is bewilderment, grief, sometimes rage and perhaps at times relief that it was not him/her. This may be difficult for the twin to acknowledge, but is understandable.

When the twins have been identical there is the issue (already touched upon) of physical presence fully represented, when in fact it is a physical *absence* that must be adjusted to. This is complicated for all of you. The bereft twin has to cope with the distressing effect of seeing his/her twin in the mirror, and knowing that s/he is a walking reminder of the deceased. During the initial stages of grief when the physical outrage of death is still fresh, this can bring about a sort of identity crisis in an identical twin. To deal with this, as said earlier, s/he must work with defining him/herself as a whole and separate person and may need help to do so. As healing takes place the mirror image becomes a greater and greater comfort. (So many bereaved parents and siblings wistfully wonder as the years pass what their child/sib would have looked like now . . .)

Generally speaking these very sensitive issues do need to be caringly confronted by family members. Pretending that they do not exist is tempting when you believe that "the less said the better". But though it may be very painful and difficult for you, if you choose the right time and are gentle with one another, you will find that the rewards make the effort well worthwhile.

9. The child who was not normal – but special

If your loss is of a child who was not normal, for instance a retardate, a Down's Syndrome or a Tay Sachs baby, a child with muscular dystrophy or cystic fibrosis, you may react in one of three ways:

● *You may feel very relieved*
If your dominant response is relief this could be for the child's sake and/or your own. When an infant is first found to be mentally or physically abnormal there is a period of grieving: you mourn the loss of a normal child with all that that means, and you question yourselves as parents. "What went wrong . . . was it our fault . . . what does it mean for the future?" It may have been very hard to accept the baby and difficult to accept yourself. Any feelings of self-condemnation that you experienced have added to your distress. If your child was severely affected you had to deal with unexpected responsibilities that perhaps, in addition to becoming a strain, made the parent-child relationship problematic. Perhaps you have ached whilst you watched your son/daughter struggle against heavy odds in a demanding world of normality.

Have you ever wondered if your child's disability was a punishment for some wrong-doing? If so, has losing him/her meant the removal of the imagined indictment, bringing a sense of (blame-laden) relief? Or does it seem as if the retribution has been doubled? If you are struggling with any such thoughts I suggest you seek counselling: you have assumed a heavy burden and have the right to request help in relinquishing it.

If time-consuming difficulties have had negative effects on your other children, you might have decided to put your disabled child in a home. Perhaps you had done so because it seemed to be in his/her best interests – but you have anguished over the decision. There are many reasons why you could be experiencing relief now that your child has died. It does not mean that you have loved less. It is very important that you accept your feelings without guilt and complete the grieving that began when the child was first found to be abnormal. Spend some time with someone with whom you can express your anger and pain.

● *You may feel grief-stricken*
You may be experiencing your child's death as an unmitigated loss to

you and your family. If so, you have been able to focus on his/her specialness and to accept any drawbacks that the disability brought. The child's extended dependency may have made you, the mother, dependent on his/her presence, in that caring has filled your time and become the centre-point upon which all other activities pivoted. Perhaps your son's/daughter's personality was expressed in a particular charm and innocence, a friendliness and quality of loving that has a special place in your heart – and leaves a gap that you do not believe can ever be filled in quite so unique a way. It is just those gifts that will in time become your comfort and bring healing as you remember them. Perhaps it is for qualities of courage, tenacity and generosity of spirit developed in response to disability, that your child is beloved. These attributes are yours to treasure and to celebrate by giving them expression in your living, on his/her behalf. Doing so will facilitate your recovery because it demonstrates how near to you your child really is: as close as your own thoughts and actions.

It is likely that your other children have been particularly close to this child because they have been able to do more for him/her and have grown protective. What an opportunity s/he has provided for learning so many valuable lessons! It is the family members' desire to shield him/her that makes the death seem such an outrage.

But equally, the dependency of the mentally or physically disabled youngster can give rise to jealousies, frustration and anger in siblings. It is so important that these feelings are discussed and no guilt is attached to them, for there are special joys and special complications attached to having such a sib, such a son/daughter.

Just as normal youngsters bring a mixture of all the delightful attributes of childhood and a handful of less attractive features as well, so do children who are not normal. They can be irritating and difficult – indeed they are "regular kids" as far as certain behaviours go. It will be a help to you all in working through your sorrow if you do not idealise your deceased child. Mourn the loss of the reality; otherwise you will find your grieving endless. It is impossible to work through fantasies.

● *You may be experiencing mixed feelings*
Many of the comments made in relation to the first two categories will be relevant. Mixed feelings are normal in grief but not easy to deal with. Insight into your responses is the first step towards sorting them out and freeing the healing process.

People may have dismissed your grief with: "I cannot imagine how you can be so upset; you are all much better off now." Such comments can be deeply hurtful, particularly as they negate the value of your child's life and your relationship with him/her. They stem from a lack of information and insight. Often fear of what is ill-understood generates such remarks. The patience to offer the speaker your perspective, if you do not feel too hurt to be compassionate, might come to the rescue of both the other person and yourself.

10. Death of an adult child

The loss of an adult son/daughter is a deeply disturbing event. The cry from parents who lost much younger children is often: "Oh, you are better off: you have had your child for so much longer. We had no time with ours." We see here intimations of some of the varied dynamics of the loss of children at different stages of life.

Indeed, the parents of an adult child *have* known a loved one for longer; this means that interconnectedness is far more complex and intricate. Separation now means the severance of a long-established relationship. The fabric of family life, many years in the weaving and accepted as lasting, is now rent. The shock and disorientation (especially if the death has been sudden and seemingly meaningless) is enormous.

I am not saying that to lose an adult child is a greater blow than the loss of a young child (or the other way around) but that different factors are involved.

Parents of adult children are generally older people: perhaps you are a little less resilient than formerly, particularly so if you have already had to cope with a great deal in your life. You may be a widow or widower and have to bear and recover from bereftness on your own. Families are so scattered these days; you may be yearning to have your members closer to you during this time.

As a parent of an adult child you had probably achieved some appropriate separateness from your son/daughter prior to the death. S/he was becoming (or already was) more independent and may have left home. In one way this could make the death a little easier to adjust to in that you are accustomed to his/her no longer living with you.

But that previous separation could make the death more difficult to cope with if you had not adapted to your son's/daughter's leaving home. Whether s/he was marrying, emigrating or whatever the circumstance was, you are now likely to be experiencing intensified grief and anger, whether acknowledged or not. You may feel cheated out of sharing the last period of your child's life. Any resentment, jealousy or blame that you hold will be sharpened by the physical finality of death.

The challenge of adjusting to an untimely loss is greater if ambivalence and/or dependency marked your relationship to him/her. Some parents can express these emotions and thoughts whilst others, feeling too vulnerable, suppress them. Unexpressed feelings intensify and if negative, fester and generate physical and/or psychological symptoms of stress. Share what you carry within so that comfort and healing can reach you. If you find it too difficult to talk, write it all down or hold a dialogue within yourself; but sharing with an understanding person is the most helpful of all.

Just when emotional resources seem drained you may be required to care for your grandchildren, themselves bereaved and in need of special comfort and understanding. The role of grandparent becomes a heart-rending one because the youngsters' distress is yours for a time. In coping with and for others you may be unable to express and work through your own pain, having to set your needs aside for the moment. If so, be sure that it *is* only temporarily. If, on the other hand, you find it impossible to be of help to others, know that this acute stage will pass, and do not accuse yourself of being weak and useless. Do the best you can, recognising that each person's pain is individual and that you must acknowledge your style and depth of mourning, energy level and coping abilities.

Perhaps you are deeply concerned and anguished for your widowed child-in-law. You might be anxious about his/her dependency on you or refusal to accept your help. Maybe you fear that s/he will move away with your grandchildren thus compounding your loss. Sometimes, however hard you try, your bereaved son/daughter-in-law resists your attentions. Painful though this may be and however much you feel that you must hold the family together for your deceased child's sake, you may have to allow his/her spouse's withdrawal. When grandchildren are involved you might be heartsore indeed if you have only limited contact with them. (See p. 91 on in-law tensions.) If there are no grandchildren you might be grieving the loss of cherished hopes and fantasies.

Sometimes (hitherto submerged?) competitiveness between you and your child-in-law manifests. Each of you hurts so much and can quite easily become possessive of the relationship with the deceased.

This not uncommon state of affairs, wounds, angers and disillusions. Try to be open-hearted: there is already so much pain. You may not be able to change someone else's views or feelings but you can take responsibility for your own – and this can be a help.

"Survivor guilt" is common in bereaved parents. Feeling outraged by your child's death you may wish that you had died instead and yet maybe, deep down, be relieved to be alive – and feel uncomfortable about that too.

Your lost hopes for your child's future are now mourned. It is as if death has cheated both him/her and you out of so many opportunities. If you had hoped that this child who is now gone would care for you in your old age you feel not only bereft but insecure as well.

Step by step these complex facets of grief can be worked through, though recovery may seem very slow in coming. Healing is brought about by recalling and reviewing with thankfulness all the years that you have shared, all that you have been able to give and to receive. This stored treasure will in time bring comfort and a sense of closeness.

11. In-law tensions after the death of a married child

If in Pandora's box there are any in-law relationship tensions such as dislikes, lack of respect, intolerance . . . the death of your son/ daughter might lift the lid right off. All of a sudden the restraining influence of your child is no longer there. In addition to your grief you have, perhaps unexpectedly, to deal with unmasked antagonism, unleashed anger. As a result, if you have grandchildren you may be permitted restricted or no access to them.

In my experience bereaved parents in this situation are shocked at the hurt and accusations that emerge. Even when no grandchildren are involved the withdrawal of the surviving spouse generally comes as a double loss. It is as if the traces of your deceased child's married life have been obliterated, and you are in a sort of no-man's land . . . You are left wondering how your child would have reacted had s/he known what would happen.

As grandparents you doubtless want the consolation of having your grandchildren close to you and you wish to comfort and sustain them. Pain and bitterness follow shock if contact is denied. Grief is compounded because they carry a part of your son/daughter within them and it seems so cruel to be threatened with losing that too.

It is important to look at these difficult and painful issues in the light of the responsibilities of each person involved. If Pandora's box is full of in-law gremlins, whether or not it is easy to ascertain and admit, each family member concerned has played a part (possibly unwittingly) in putting them there. Blame-tagging is not the issue: the point is that each of you have it in your power to resolve the difficulties. The key factor is the flexibility and the honest desire to do so. Protestations of innocence on anyone's part may indicate that that person is unaware or unwilling to see how his/her behaviour has been perceived.

Such situations can be resolved in either of two ways:
- □ by sharing responsibility for them – a genuine and mutual readiness to make amends, or
- □ in the absence of agreement, by your willingness to use this opportunity for limit-setting coupled with forgiveness. This rules out punitive measures and revenge.

Limit-setting may be effective in halting unacceptable behaviour (e.g.: "I cannot allow you to treat us in this way"). Whether it is helpful or not, you will have to set constraints upon any negativity in your own attitude and responses. This is actually what response-ability is all about. You have your personal ethics and integrity. Even if someone's conduct does not match up to them, do not allow your own standards to fall. Whether or not that effects change in anyone else, it does ensure that you do not get caught up in recriminations and other destructiveness.

Forgiveness is also vital. It may seem as much as you can do to restrain yourself from retaliation; but if you can manage that extra step of grace, you will find that the resultant inner tranquility and sense of resolution is well worth the effort.

What I am saying here can best be summed up in the challenging question: "Can you be bigger than small?" Can you find release from the bondage of ill feeling?

If you are unable to convey your love to your grandchildren and are haunted by the thought that they will think you have deserted them, perhaps you can write to them, tactfully and caringly. Possibly a middle-man can solve the communication difficulty.

The situation may seem unendurable at times. Learn to express your feelings in ways that do not hurt others but bring you relief. There is so much negativity and stress these days. Dare we do anything other than deal creatively with our own? Allowing healing to replace suffering brings its own rewards. When optimal solutions are not possible, you can still find peace. Two practical ways through which you might find restoration are the (further) development of a prayer life, and helping people in need. But caring for yourself as a mourner must come before or, when you are ready, be simultaneous with caring for others. There is no wisdom in the premature replacement of self-nurture.

12. For grandparents

With the death of a grandchild you carry a threefold pain: you grieve on the grandchild's behalf – s/he has had so little time to live and has had to relinquish all the opportunities the future here held; you ache, sometimes beyond words, for the suffering of your children and your spouse, and you mourn your own great loss. All this love and compassion mounts and leaves you feeling helpless, angry and so deeply distressed.

Many grandparents have told me they would gladly have died in their grandchild's stead; that they have overstayed their welcome here, having lived through many of life's stages and in some cases are even ready to die. To some of these older family members their children's anguish seems almost accusatory and they assume guilt for surviving.

Perhaps it would be useful to look at your anguish, your grief as it affects and is affected by your family relationships, how you can be of assistance to your grieving children, and finally, some additional ways in which you may find comfort.

Some grandparents are on excellent terms with their families whilst others are not. I address both situations.

● *Your anguish*
Here I am only going to outline common reactions, specific to grandparents. On p. 147 you will find a description of the grief experience.

☐ *A feeling of desolation and helplessness* perhaps related to:
  ☐ not having been able to prevent the death
  ☐ not being able to cope better with your own grief
  ☐ not being able to give more comfort to your children
  ☐ not having any answers for them
  ☐ perhaps having given wrong advice . . .
  ☐ not having recognised signs/symptoms earlier

☐ accepting care from others
☐ still being alive . . .

☐ *Self-blame* in relation to the above factors. It is so easy when grieving to forget that you are fallible and to assume guilt for what was beyond your control.

In relation to the last two factors the following:
☐ You have the right to accept help, indeed are wise to do so.
☐ It may give you added strength to be of assistance to the grieving parents.
☐ The fact that you have survived your grandchild presumably means that you have not yet completed what you are here on earth to do. Whatever his/her circumstance, it is not given to you to decide that you should have gone in his/her stead.

☐ *A desire to be supportive and of practical help.* Your attempts may be welcomed or unwelcome, at times successful, at times not. They may lead to your feeling valued or to a sense of uselessness, frustration, impotence. For quite a time grief distorts perspective, judgement and general clarity of thinking. Emotions have no logic and so flexibility and resilience are required of anyone wanting to be of assistance.

☐ *Anger at the loss* to you and what it has done to all your loved ones and, perhaps (by association and vulnerable as you are at present) an emphasis on past angers. Try not to get involved with attitudes or issues that rankle. With sensitivity heightened as it is now, you will only do harm by spotlighting problems.

☐ *A loving desire to protect your family members.* You may already have gone through a great loss and know how difficult a road lies ahead.

☐ *A sense of having suddenly aged.* In time and with self-care and healing this will change for the better.

● *Family relationships*
Let us consider your affiliation with your child and son/daughter-in-law: Are you close to them both, only to one of them, or to neither? Were you close to your deceased grandson/daughter and how have your children viewed your relationship?

If you, your children and grandchildren have enjoyed warm interactions you are able to offer comfort and support insofar as you can share in their grief without burdening them with your own. You are in a delicate position: they need to be able to turn to you for consolation, know that you too mourn deeply, and yet not feel that they must be responsible for comforting you. (So often grandparents feel that they are the forgotten ones, partly for the above reason and because the bereaved parents are naturally seen as the chief mourners. Concern of others is often not extended beyond caring for them.)

A time of mourning is not ideal for resolving difficulties and misunderstandings. If your relationship with your family has not been an affirming one you may be faced now with some complicated issues. Perhaps you are needed and included by some members and not by others. With feelings (your own included) being raw and extra-sensitive at this time the wisest thing to do may be to ask for guidance as to how best you can fit in. This may seem to ignore your needs for comfort, but being there when appropriate, and giving space when not, must surely improve relations and thus be of some consolation to you.

If you have a serious family rift this might be an opportunity to heal it, just because everyone is in such need of solace. It is surely worth attempting to reunite with your children, but if that is not possible you must take care of yourself by trying to resolve the various griefs that you carry. I will return to the subject of comfort at the end of this section.

● *To be of assistance*
☐ As you know, there is great value in
  ☐ spending time listening without judgement to what your grieving children and grandchildren need to say;
  ☐ offering the supportive love that allows each one the space to mourn in his/her own way; and
  ☐ providing an encompassing quietness that makes no demands.

☐ You are probably already taking care of the practicalities of daily living – the shopping, planning and cooking of meals, taking and fetching the children as necessary – these are an invaluable help.

☐ If you do not live nearby or are not in a state of health to take on tasks, supportive messages and personal tokens of your love provide great comfort. You will find there are other ways in which you can help: ask your family for guidance and make your own suggestions to them if you are unsure where the most immediate needs lie.

☐ Take care of your own health. You are probably putting the needs of your family before your own and getting exhausted.

● *Additional ways in which to find comfort*
To wish to take on the suffering of others is of no help to anyone. Putting your life experience to creative use in your own style will bear fruit and you will be effective. Expressing feelings of redundancy or of being in the way are a drain on your grieving children. Perhaps a visit to your minister will give you renewed strength and some perspective that may sustain you and your family.

Answer needs rather than questioning life, after a death has occurred. Can you work with your faith in the face of loss? Do you have a philosophy of life that you can draw on and extend?

All that has been said about the value of the appropriate expression of grief applies to you as well. Even though you may be spending a great deal of time with your children and grandchildren, make time to be with those of your friends who will comfort you.

Again, pay attention to your health during this stressful period; neglecting to eat or getting insufficient sleep can only take a toll. Visit your doctor or homeopath if you feel you need his/her help and explain that you are bereaved.

If you are feeling worried about your grieving or that of any of your family members you may find that a visit to a counsellor brings some relief and welcome guidance. The future without your grandson/ -daughter may seem bleak indeed, so pain-filled that it seems hardly worth going on. Indeed suicidal thoughts are not uncommon in mourners, but seeking help is the answer. Healing is natural but you have to give it time.

13. Friends and loss

Bereaved parents often complain that many of their friends either avoid them after the death of a child, or do not know what to say or how to listen to them. I am addressing this section to you, the mourners. There is frequently a great deal of hurt in you who feel rejected or misunderstood. I trust that your friends will read this too, but it is generally you who are bruised or angry and who have to take the initiative to make visitors feel at ease.

Death is still to some extent a taboo subject, and the loss of a child is a very threatening event. When fear and confusion are the main responses, avoidance may be the chosen behaviour. Although you react to this with anger and distress, thinking that your companions could well put their feelings aside and consider your needs, it may be precisely their recognition of your pain and bereftness that keeps them away.

No doubt some people do find it hard to put themselves in others' shoes. Their evasion may be due to insensitivity, insecurity, self-consciousness or inexperience. Superstitious fears form a barrier too, whilst a sort of embarrassment at being so fortunate as not to be bereaved can engender fear of the mourners' envy. What a need there is for information to bridge the divide!

In our society we actually have no code of behaviour nor etiquette for confronting the bereaved. Nervousness blocks many spontaneous gestures of consolation. There is the desire to withdraw and escape – just as you wish you could from your pain. Friends can and you cannot. Therein lies the source of much of your anger – with unresponsive or inappropriately responsive people, the avoiders, the curious, the tactless, the threatened . . .

Barriers that exist between the bereaved and their friends are created by the latter's attempts to deny feelings in order to protect the bereaved. Common rationalisations are: "They need to be alone"; "It will upset them to talk about their pain"; "I'm afraid I'll say the wrong thing or cry".

- *How can you help both them and yourself?*
  - ☐ Realise that caring rather than non-caring is very often behind the avoidance.
  - ☐ Try not to take the errors of judgement personally.
  - ☐ Be non-judgemental: criticism can only do harm.
  - ☐ Recognize that you have made the same mistakes.
  - ☐ Tell them what you need: e.g. that it is alright to mention your deceased child and you want to talk about him/her.
  - ☐ Be prepared to take the initiative in conversations.
  - ☐ Re-establish contact with valued friends.
  - ☐ Realise that this gets more difficult as time goes by, therefore act now.
  - ☐ Put your healing before your hurt feelings. You have lost enough. Do all that you can when you can to make life meaningful again.

Do not be afraid to tell friends how you feel when they invite you out and you do not wish to go. Ask them to bear with you. Do what you feel suits you best (perhaps you have to make compromises with your spouse at times). Reassure them (and yourself) that the time will come when you will be glad to accept invitations again.

There are so many wonderful companions who over the months put themselves out to really listen, be supportive, comforting and helpful – they need mention too. Rich is their reward in knowing that they have been able to make an appreciable difference during your darkest hours of grief.

How to cope . . .

D With grief related to cause of death

1. Miscarriage and grief

There are parents who welcome a miscarriage because for some reason the pregnancy has not been well-received. However, this section is addressed to those who, when the loss occurs, experience deep disappointment, bereftness and despair. A miscarriage means losing your live baby in embryo, and having to give up all attendant hopes and plans. When this goes unrecognised you cannot grieve appropriately: it is not possible to work through what seems unreal and you cannot mourn in isolation.

We live in community with others and need to share both the events we celebrate and those which cause us anguish.

With the confirmation of the pregnancy a reality develops. Though at first you may keep it a private delight, a warm secret, it becomes as the weeks pass, a mutual anticipation. Part of the joy is in sharing the happiness, the preparation and plans.

With the miscarriage all this is lost, and there has been but a brief time of anticipation. Your depression, pain and the loss of creativity must also be recognised and shared. It is not only you who must acknowledge and work through the grief (and you might be feeling that you do not have the right to mourn) but you need the participation of your family members and friends as well.

● *What does this miscarriage represent to you?*
☐ Loss of proof of the ability to carry and nurture a foetus to full term – i.e. a loss of trust in your own body? When it has been difficult to become pregnant and when the cause of the miscarriage is unclear, there are distressing misgivings, self-mistrust and self-blame that are hard to deal with. Even knowing the reason for the loss of the pregnancy might not allay your worries and present sense of failure.

☐ Deprivation of a physical part of yourself? The unborn child is so personal an entity for a mother that your feelings run deep – a fact perhaps not fully understood by your partner.

● *The mother's grief reactions to miscarriage*

☐ There is the shock, the desperate need to halt the process of separation and the grief when that is not possible. The effects of the disbelief and denial that often follow it (particularly if you did not see the foetus), might manifest in the belief that you are still pregnant and in searching for your baby. You may not want to leave the hospital without him/her.

Some of the most common symptoms are pining, forgetfulness, odd behaviour at times and a fear that you are going crazy. In addition, a see-sawing of emotions (contributed to by hormonal changes and the shock to your body of the termination of pregnancy) and extreme sensitivity.

If you have had repeated miscarriages your sense of failure and inadequacy will be stronger – particularly if you have not yet brought a baby to full term.

The sense of isolation when it seems as if no-one else is grieving, and comments such as: "You'll have another one", "You didn't even know the baby" and "It's better this way", indicate to you that there is a lack of understanding – a lonely feeling that might leave you both sad and angry.

You are in need of as much information, realistic encouragement, loving affirmation and support as can be given. Try, in addition to your desire for a successful pregnancy, to give attention to other meaningful activities.

● *The father's reactions to miscarriage*

The father of this lost infant, has not experienced the intimacy of pregnancy and may find it hard to empathise with his partner's feelings. In addition, men and women tend to grieve differently owing to differences in personality, temperament, and to societal expectations.

What is expected from a man, may cramp his natural desire to acknowledge the enormity of his loss and to grieve about it. Accept the courage of your convictions; you will find not only relief but probably some rewarding recognition to boot! ("The Grief Experience" on p. 147 may be useful to you.)

Miscarriage, like any other significant loss, puts a strain on a relationship and it is important therefore to take care. ("Marriage and Loss" on p. 66 deals with this issue.)

● **Should we tell our other children about the miscarriage?**
The answers to the questions whether, and if so how, to tell your children about the loss are individual to each family.

☐ *Some general guidelines that may help:*

☐ If the miscarriage occurred very early on in pregnancy and the other children did not know that a baby was expected, you might want to say nothing and have no questions and distress to deal with. But you have to take your grief into account: your children will be aware of and disturbed by it.

☐ It might be better to give youngsters a simple and honest explanation that the baby that was on the way was not able to continue growing and so died and is no longer inside mummy. You may want to follow this with the reassurance that you are alright though very sad, and you can all mourn and recover together. Younger children generally accept that they can be told more when they are older.

☐ Decide what and how much information is suitable for the older ones according to their temperaments and maturity. Say nothing that will later have to be unsaid, and when you do not know the answers to their questions do not be afraid to say so. (Part II deals with the grief of children.)

The acknowledgement of your loss (by you and by others), the expression of your grief, and the allowing of enough time to work through it all, bring about the reintegration you seek. Medical reassurance, hope for a full-term pregnancy, and the intention to begin again in the near future help, but should not displace your mourning. Grief not appropriately dealt with is stored.

Rites that underline the reality of your lost foetus are a great help; all the usual proof of a death such as a service and burial, newspaper announcements, etc. are missing. You can name your child even if you do not know the sex. You could make a scrap-book with poems or an account of your experience, a letter to your infant, some pressed flowers or pictures – whatever appeals to you. Perhaps you would rather plant a special shrub or tree in his/her memory. Whatever you decide to do, share it with others who will really listen to you and honour the short life that was lived. (In the list given at the end of this book you will find some titles that may be of interest to you.)

2. Abortion, ectopic pregnancy and the death of the mother

Spontaneous abortion was discussed in the previous article. Here I will discuss grief related to chosen or prescribed abortion.

● *Grief related to abortion*
The extent to which the developing infant is welcome, and the reason for its abortion, will have a great deal to do with your response to the loss. There may be relief or an overwhelming sense of disappointment, even despair. Perhaps on testing your baby was found to be defective; maybe s/he died in utero and had to be removed.

The matter is a delicate one, having moral, religious and legal connotations. This means that in addition to having to cope with losing a foetus, you are faced with wider implications. Even when abortion was medically prescribed, because of your religious belief it might be difficult to reconcile the act with the ethics thereof.

Maybe women's rights are an issue for you with regard to intervening in an unwanted pregnancy. Feeling rebellious and assertive when up against the law of the country, you are dealing with the loss of freedom to make decisions for yourself and your family.

If the procedure was done by a less than competent person you may be having to cope with physical damage, sterility – and anger, desperation and condemnation.

It is clear that abortion is a complex issue and the responses to it are varied and deep.

Even if you feel the medical verdict was correct and unavoidable you will still grieve the resultant loss. Whilst it might have been a relief to have the doctor take the decision out of your hands, you may struggle with anger directed at him/her – and feel that you are being unreasonable and ungrateful. In the midst of confusion do not be unfair to yourself. Give yourself time to regain perspective.

Perhaps you are amongst people who do not condone abortion, or who want a child and cannot conceive . . . If so, you might be feeling uncomfortable, guilty, misunderstood and unsupported. Having to keep the subject and therefore your grief private is no help in working through it.

When genetic factors or age have been responsible for the decision to have an abortion, in addition to self-blame (how lonely and unhappy you must be feeling) there may be unexpressed or explicit accusations between you and your partner. Adequacy and accountability are questioned and it is so easy for a wedge to be driven between the two of you. (Please read "Marriage and loss" on p. 66.)

Telling your children sad news has briefly been dealt with previously, and children's grief is the subject following.

What does have to be touched upon here is the matter of conflict within or between you in relation to the abortion. Before talking to your family to try to resolve the issue for yourselves; if this is not possible at the moment then an agreed-upon compromise, at least with regard to what will be told them, is a good second-best solution.

Clearly, to have counselling may be wise. There are many factors to cope with at a time when you are faced with all the normal reactions to loss. By this I do not imply that without help you will not manage your grieving successfully; but counselling is a guide, a support and shortens the mourning period.

Loss of a foetus is not a minor event: it affects you, your spouse and your family for quite some time.

● *Grief and ectopic pregnancy*
Fertilisation of the ovum in the fallopian tube (which runs from each ovary into the uterus) or in the abdomen itself, is called an ectopic pregnancy. Because of the risk to you, the embryo must immediately be surgically removed on diagnosis. Concern for your safety and recovery usually masks the grief, but the loss of both the pregnancy and a damaged tube must be mourned. Because of the emergency, the sudden unexpected shock and the loss, you will need time for your emotional recovery; time to be, rather than to be doing. You are given the coping abilities for the adjustments that you have to make, but need to set the pace that is right for you. Recognise your grief and work through it. Knowing how fortunate you are to have had the operation in good time must not deny you the right to mourn.

● *Loss of the mother*
Perhaps an abortion whether spontaneous, chosen, prescribed or an operation for her ectopic pregnancy has caused the death of the mother – your wife/partner. Profound regret and anguish follow so great a loss. You may be enraged at her for agreeing to the intervention, at the doctor who was involved, at yourself for not having been able to prevent her death – or even for having fathered the child. God may be the target if you are angry. Does the desperate sense of helplessness and wanting to turn the clock back seem to be driving you crazy?

All these feelings and many more are normal under the circumstances, but must be acknowledged and expressed.

If you are having difficulties in relation to family members, whether children, in-laws . . . get help. You cannot be expected to successfully deal with all your and other peoples' emotions at the same time – and particularly not if there is antagonism present.

There are a number of sections in this book that will be useful to you.

3. Grieving a stillbirth or neonatal death

Grief at the death of an infant is accompanied by seemingly unbearable disappointment, and the stark contrast between the creativity of pregnancy and loss of a future containing that child. Having no memories other than those of being pregnant and the quickening in the womb, your grief is difficult to work through. It is almost as if that longed-for baby has never been. Relatives and friends may perceive the child as a non-person and instead of being supportive may encourage you to distract yourself, forget and get on with life.

● *Advice to the mother*
It is most important to keep communication lines open between you and your family members and the professionals able to help you. Do not be afraid to talk about your baby, your dashed hopes; the worries that you have. The confusion and questions about cause of death, future pregnancies and genetic factors need to be verbalised and responded to.

Perhaps you are worrying that this loss was a punishment . . . Self-blame is self-torture and the accusations you make against yourself are probably groundless. Certainly God does not take children as retribution for wrongdoing. If this issue is troubling you deeply, speak to your minister about it.

Do not block your tears, anger, desperation, misgivings, feelings of having failed your baby and one another.

Grief is so intense an experience; you may feel for quite some time that you are dislocated from your usual self or going crazy. It is frightening to feel like this. The fruitless searching for your infant, the pain at seeing other parents with babies, having to dry up precious milk, the ache of empty arms and the loneliness of crying – all these are normal reactions, amongst many others. They will subside and pass in time. Take care to do what you feel is most comforting and healing.

I suggest that if you have not already done so, you name your son/daughter. Make that child real in your own mind and for others in any way that you are able to. You cannot mourn a shadow. Your baby lived, and if you are fortunate in having a photograph, a wrist bracelet from the hospital, a footprint or handprint on paper, the birth and death certificates – these will give substance to the reality and are aids to mourning. In addition or instead I encourage you to write him/her a poem or letter in which you express all that you would like to say, honouring the bond that exists between you even though you have had to say goodbye so soon.

If there has been no funeral for your baby do consider holding a memorial service or making some commemorative gesture such as lighting a candle and offering a prayer for your child, planting a tree in his/her memory or making a donation in his/her name.

● *Advice to the father*
You might be one of the fathers who find it hard to relate to a stillborn or neonatally-lost baby. If you were not able to bond with your developing infant during the pregnancy there might now be a gulf of misunderstandings between you and your wife. Perhaps you had loved your baby from the start and are now grieving deeply as a couple.

Or is it "business as usual" – and you do not know what to do with your pain? Separate grief can interfere with your marital relationship. Both physically and emotionally (due to the effects of distress and the mother's hormonal balance not yet having been re-established) you and she are likely to be out of step.

This is a time when you both need to be able to draw close, offer consolation, support and give one another permission to have his/her own responses to the loss. (There is a relevant section on marriage on p. 66 and others that address these difficulties.)

Perhaps practically you have not known what to do for the best: should the prepared nursery items be cleared away to avoid pain or left in place for your wife to do with as she wishes? Generally the wisest course to follow is to ask her what she would prefer.

Ideally, mutual agreement should be reached about what and how to tell the children. (The section following this one should be of some assistance to you.)

Because mourning is a process and healing (if not interfered with) takes place naturally, there is no need for either of you to despair, however desperate you are feeling. Try to have patience whilst taking care of yourselves and of each other. Coping with all of this is by no means easy but it is possible to emerge from the experience and find life meaningful together once more.

4. Grieving a cot death

The unexpected cot death of an apparently healthy, normal baby throws you into grief fraught with terrified questions, self-accusation and an icy sense of guilt. Being faced with the police when you are acutely vulnerable and have a desperate need for privacy, compounds the nightmare.

It is likely that you are feeling overwhelmingly insecure and incompetent as a parent. For a time you will experience a sense of powerlessness and panic; your emotions will become physical pain and pressure. There is a strong desire to escape the anguish and the torment of recurring images. You may be holding on to your routine, going almost automatically through your daily tasks, just to maintain some semblance of normality in the midst of the emptiness and seemingly crazy thoughts. Perhaps you are turning to some crutch such as alcohol or tranquillizers. (See p. 20 if that is so.) Repeatedly talking about your feelings and disturbing visions will help you to work through them and heal.

It is very hard to cope with an unexplained tragedy and as yet research has not found the cause of cot death. Agonized by questions and self-blame, fearing that you killed your baby, haunted by feelings of failure, you seek relief and yet there seem to be so few answers. Having a reason for what has occurred would give you some sense of control.

Your fears (many of them irrational) and your self-condemnation need expression if you are to cope. As soon as possible your goal must be to set them aside, although this is very difficult: it is almost as if you have to castigate yourself in the face of such a loss.

Your grief requires an outlet and cannot be set aside. You will be able to work through it in time.

In the midst of the mixed disbelief and cold realisation you also have to deal with the reactions of those around you. Many parents have said after a cot death that they want to hide to avoid any reproaches and questions from others – even the unverbalised insinuations they infer from the way people are looking at them. It is a time of such acute sensitivity. Family and friends in their bewilderment, supportive though they wish to be, may come with misleading theories and even thoughtless remarks.

The Cot Death Society in Cape Town published an excellent leaflet which gives you the information that you need to allay your fears. The addresses from where it can be obtained are given at the end of this section.

Thus far in South Africa it is only in the Cape that the term "Death due to natural causes" followed by "cot death" or "Sudden Infant Death Syndrome" (SIDS) is entered on the death certificate. Elsewhere in the Republic the cause of death is usually given as cerebral vascular accident (CVA), or suffocation.

These labels intensify distress: cot deaths are not caused by an accident nor by asphyxiation or suffocation. Such terms are not only misleading but imply that you, and/or whoever was care-taking at the time, was responsible for the death of your child. "Natural causes: cot death" may leave you wondering what that means, but it does make it clear that you have not actively caused your baby's demise.

The police investigation of the death, the post mortem and the inquest (when required) to establish cause, whilst exceedingly difficult to cope with, are for your protection. If sensitively handled, they can bring you some peace of mind as far as your non-culpability is concerned. Perhaps at the time all that you are aware of is that you feel under suspicion. Nevertheless in time you may be grateful that an inquiry was conducted.

How painful to have to identify your baby. If you want to spend some time with him/her do not be afraid to ask. Having had the child removed from your care straight after death may have left you feeling that your son/daughter was no longer yours. Affirm the bond between the two of you in any way that you can. You have not done violence to your baby: the death could not have been prevented. You have the right to hold your child, whether physically or within your heart, and pour out your love.

The decision of what to do with his/her things is a matter of personal preference. You might wish to leave everything in its place for the time being, or think it best to pack it all away. Obviously the decision rests to quite an extent on whether you intend to have another baby or not. Maybe you would like to lend some of the items to family or friends in the meanwhile. There is no hurry to dispose of clothing, toys or anything else. Deal with them when you feel ready.

Having suffered a bereavement in this way you will naturally be anxious about having another baby. For some the idea is unthinkable for a long time, whilst most couples want to fill the gap in their lives as soon as possible. This desire is complicated by fear of another cot death and feelings of inadequacy as a parent. But overriding all else is the need to hold an infant close, to nurture again.

To protect yourself against your next child becoming a replacement baby (to the extent that the following pregnancy interferes with your mourning), you might like to make a journal or a scrapbook documenting the life of the child you have lost. Your experiences, pictures, poems, anecdotes, contributions from your spouse and children – they all go to make up that child's story. You can then make a separate record of your experiences of the next pregnancy, birth and babyhood. (Please read the sections on stress and marriage on p. 66 and if you have other children, on children's grief in Part II.)

The undermining of your self-concept as a capable adult, as a marriage partner and as a parent can seriously affect all your relationships. Dealing with the effects of a cot death entails more than working through grief: it means having to re-establish your sense of yourself as a valuable and competent human being. It may be wise to seek counselling for support and perspective. If you feel you want to talk to other parents who have been through a cot death ordeal The Cot Death Society or The Compassionate Friends will be able to put you in touch with them.

The Cot Death Society leaflet is available from:
Ms Jane Brown, The Cot Death Society, PO Box 11306, Vlaeberg 8012. Tel day: (021) 408-6922.
The Compassionate Friends, PO Box 46305, Orange Grove 2119, Johannesburg. Tel. all hours (011) 728-4451.

5. Death after illness

● *The mother's grief*
As a mother you have cared for, worried about, sustained and comforted your child. You have had consultations with doctors and spent long hours at the hospital. You have coped somehow with a sick child, meals, household shopping and tried to meet your husband's and your children's needs. You have wept and been brave, felt you could go on no longer and yet have been a source of continued strength and comfort.

And now, with your child gone, your arms, heart, days and nights all feel so empty. Your dying child filled your life. Now it seems you have no energy left to help anyone or to care so deeply ever again. Perhaps it feels as if your labour of love has been in vain; yet maybe there is some sense of fulfilment in knowing you could do no more than your utmost – and is that not what you have done even under such difficult circumstances?

Maybe there is relief at the liberation from suffering. Your pain, disbelief, and longing will all take their course and in time give way to healing as will the anger that may be demanding expression, making you tense. You are likely to be exhausted and "if only's" may creep up on you. Take care of yourself and try to rest. Think of all the times when you were able to bring comfort. Can you now spend some time alone? There is value in solitude, as well as in sharing grief and in being distracted from it.

● *The father's grief*
How hard it must have been for you, the father, to concentrate on your job knowing that your child was dying. How difficult to realise your wife was striving to manage whilst filled with anticipatory mourning; your children anxious and distressed. You may have longed to spend more time with your family, and your sick child in particular.

Perhaps you have felt guilty at being able to escape into your work. What mixed feelings there are when life/death issues are to be borne!

Anger, a sense of impotence at not having been able to save your son/daughter, at having given life and having had to countenance its slipping away . . . These thoughts and feelings raise the anguished question: Why? It is all so painful, and you may be feeling helpless, unable to comfort yourself or your grieving family.

Do not segregate yourself. The anguish must somehow be faced and shared for healing to take place. Protecting yourself behind ongoing silence only isolates. Some people find it very difficult to cry, to articulate their pain. If you are one of them, be prepared to listen whenever you are able to, for often what is said (in addition to bringing relief to the speaker) is a verbalisation for you and therefore helpful. Perhaps you can write your thoughts and feelings down. That too can be of value.

You have all been through "trial by fire" and no doubt have learned a great deal and regretted many things. You have railed, wept, blamed yourselves, felt beaten and had victories. Because the death in your family has not come entirely unexpectedly and suddenly, you have had time to care for your loved one, to resolve difficulties there may have been between you, to express love and say goodbye. Maybe you feel there is so much that is still unfinished, that you regret having said or done, or having omitted to say or do . . . Maybe you never did manage to say goodbye.

It is never too late to tell your child whatever you need to. Hold him/her close in your mind and heart, speak of your love and your grief. When you are ready you will be able to say your farewells.

You are still a family unit though all seems changed. It is your time now to work through your pain, day by day, taking care of yourself and, to the extent that you can, of one another. Give thanks both for that which you had and still have. Try not to let your huge sense of loss fill your lives to the negation of your present relationships. It is possible to come through a period of mourning with greater closeness as a family, if you so desire.

To those who have lost an only child through illness, you and your spouse do have each other. Whilst your lives may seem empty and meaningless since the death, just keeping going will give you the time to discover that life can again become meaningful. Would your child not want you to find it so? (On p. 76 and p. 79 you will find sections on the loss of an only child.)

You are not alone. Many have walked your path. You, like them, will come through ready to accept life's opportunities and challenges once more – if that is what you desire. A section addresses single parents on p. 73.

6. Homosexuality, AIDS and bereavement

AIDS is generally associated with homosexuality. One of your first reactions when told that your child had the disease, might have been concern as to whether he was gay. This would have been coupled with the shock of the life sentence that the disease syndrome presented. In addition you might have experienced great distress at not having known before if your child *was* homosexual.

Perhaps you did know and had accepted it. Or maybe you had known and rejected him and were now facing a double loss – that of your privacy and of your son. Here was your opportunity to encompass him and gain in spite of your difficulty with his style of living.

A young man being gay, may fear rejection from his family and therefore not tell his parents until AIDS exposes his personal preferences. To some extent there would have been estrangement if he felt, rightly or wrongly, that so central an aspect of his life had to be hidden, protected.

If this was the situation you may have deeply regretted the valuable time wasted, been filled with sorrow and questioned why your child had not told you before that he was gay.

This is a complicated issue. Homosexuality raises questions in parents about the quality of their parenting and, going deeper, about themselves as people. "To what extent was this my fault?" is the worry.

Most important is not to lose sight of the individual, your child, whatever choices he made. To the extent that you have had difficulty with the fact of his sexual preferences, there is specific grief work that you need to do to enable you to complete your grieving. This relates to loving your son even if what he did is hard for you to accept. Being and doing are, after all, not the same. To mourn fully means endeavouring to deny no aspect of your child or his life. This can present difficulties for you if you feel exposed and ashamed of his homosexuality and of being his parent.

If, during his illness you have been at his side, consoling and sharing, you will have derived great comfort. During that time you might have been able to by-pass most problems regarding his particular choices.

But now the nature of his death perhaps causes you to wonder about judgement, punishment . . . Certainly it is not for us to judge another. Can you find and/or maintain faith in a God of unconditional love, and trust that all is in His care?

If that challenges you because it is so difficult, even seemingly impossible, can you work with it through prayer and meditation nevertheless?

Anger that might have been held at bay during the illness may now be directed towards your child for contracting AIDS and for dying. From this point of view he, not only his death, has become the cause of your anguish. These feelings are understandable and need alleviation. A most healing route to take is the one through forgiveness. You want your son restored to you in the sense of his acceptability . . . the memories untarnished by judgementalism or by the disease. (See the sections on forgiveness on p. 48, and restoration on p. 52.)

111

Because your child died of AIDS you may find that there is less support and consolation offered you by family and friends than would have been the case if the cause of death had been different. There is so much ignorance about the illness, so many fears and therefore still some stigma attached to it. As a result perhaps you are having to deal with avoidance by others – if not of you, of the subject of your son's death. If so, how hard that must be! Broach the subject when you wish to; you may find that by confronting the fears, barriers are broken down. Do not be afraid to tell people what your needs are and to ask for comfort. From amongst the network of befrienders you may have found the enrichment of new friendships. Their support can mean so much.

What about your son's partner, if he had someone special sharing his life? Are you able to offer him acceptance? He, too, is grieving. Whilst dealing with your own pain there is little energy left over for others, but are you able to include him in the last rites, and honour any final wishes your child may have had? Perhaps you are including this partner as a member of your now extended family.

It requires great sensitivity and fairness on both sides when it comes to sharing your son's effects. If he had an established relationship with someone, the contents of their home may be jointly theirs. It might be particularly difficult if you have only recently had your child come back into your life, not to hold fast to whatever was his. There may seem to be so little substance to the parent-child relationship if you have not been close.

Going back to your earliest memories of him and recalling him with love through all the stages of his growth may give you back your sense of connectedness.

7. Accidental death and grief

All fatal accidents fall into the category of unexpected death, which entails extreme shock, disbelief, helplessness, abandonment and victimisation. You have probably experienced a feeling of being dislocated, removed. Sudden death brings insecurity in its wake and a desire to escape reality. Anger rages at the apparent senselessness and unfairness and if the end has been violent and/or due to negligence, it knows no bounds.

Self-accusation and feelings of guilt seem almost always to be associated with accidental death, even when the mourner has not had anything directly to do with it. The greater the sense of devastation the more persistent the self-blame, the "if only's".

You may think (rightly or wrongly) that you were directly responsible for the accident that took your child's life. Perhaps you are being blamed (again, rightly or wrongly). As a result you may see yourself as a murderer. You did not murder your child. Homicide involves deliberate intent.

As human beings we are all fallible. How many times has every parent, yourself included, made a mistake – even one that should not have been made – been careless and got away with it? If you were responsible for the accident you were most unfortunate this time and suffer the terrible consequences. Is the loss not sufficient punishment? Do you need self-recrimination as well?

It will perhaps take you quite a while to be able to stop accusing and to focus on forgiving yourself for being falible. Please seek help if you are agonizing over your accountability for your child's death.

Sometimes parents or members of the family want to be told the details of the accident, whilst others shun all information. If you were not present, knowing what had happened may help you to feel more a part of your child's last moments, whereas avoidance can spare you some of the pain. Each mourner must be allowed to decide for him/herself what his/her needs are.

Three additional and important areas of difficulty for the suddenly bereaved come to mind:

☐ *Unfinished business:* There have been no good-byes, no reaching of completion . . . Without warning so much is left undone, unsaid. But even after a death has occurred it is not too late to tell your son/daughter all that you want to.

☐ *Survivor guilt:* "What right have I to go on living when s/he is dead?" It is not in chronological order to have your child die before you. It takes time to realise that there is still much for you to do – perhaps in your child's name.

☐ *The necessary intrusion of law officials and the press:* When you feel raw and vulnerable, your privacy is invaded. You may recognise that the role the police play is vital, yet immediately after an accident their investigations bring home the reality you are not yet ready to deal with. You might feel that they make certain implications with which you cannot cope. Fortunately sub-conscious defences do help to protect you from what could be overwhelming.

Perhaps you are tortured by the thought that your child might have suffered before dying. Shock anaesthetizes pain and distress for quite a while. If death came relatively quickly there would not have been any such awareness. Some of you may know that your son/daughter suffered: s/he is now beyond that and it has no further relevance for him/her. Try to resist the suppositions or imaginings about pain; you have enough to contend with.

After a road accident thoughts about a life needlessly and senselessly wasted are intensified by anger against your child if it was his/her fault. Driving without a licence, after being forbidden to, or careless handling of a motor-cycle . . . it seems youngsters cannot be protected from their own wilfulness and vulnerability and now you too are suffering. If the accident was not your child's fault your anger is likely to be even greater. Too late to be able to protect, how tense and anxious you become, how disturbed by other accidents whether real or portrayed by the media. Heightened sensitivity renders you emotionally vulnerable and affects your daily life. You may be feeling suicidal in your grief; yet mourning is a process and step by step you will be able to come through.

When death was caused by a shooting accident or by falling you may be troubled by the possibility of it having been suicide. All the evidence possible must be gathered to establish the actual cause of death. Sometimes it is difficult to be sure. If you believe that your child died by accident it is generally inappropriate for anyone to impose an alternative cause of death upon you.

You might be experiencing almost ungovernable rage against the Defence Force if it is implicated in the shooting. This is a situation in which you may have to endure a sense of almost total impotence in your endeavours to get information. The grieving process is extended by the waiting, the immense frustration involved and the institutionalisation of the death. All this has the effect of negating your need for some recognition of the value of your son's life.

The shooting may have been a civilian tragedy. The person responsible, gunsmiths, anyone who could have even remotely been to blame, become the targets of your anger. Whether justified or not, it must be worked through.

It is a nightmare to come upon the scene of an accidental death. If you were present then or shortly afterwards you may have to work through haunting visualisations. If they are constantly recurring your mind has not been able to come to terms with them; you need repeatedly to talk them through until they cease causing you such anguish.

When a child chokes, the parents, particularly if they were there, feel they should have been able to prevent it or to successfully intervene. Part of the torture of grief after an accidental death is the helplessness and the self-recriminations. There is the conviction that it should not have occurred. How desperate a thought that is! It takes time to get beyond the sense of inadequacy as a parent that often accompanies this type of death; it takes time and sharing with someone who understands and will listen to get beyond the nightmares.

Death from asthma, like choking, leaves you feeling impotent and horrified. You, like many parents, probably did not realise that it could be a fatal condition and this will leave you with distressing self-blame and questioning. (The sections on anger, p. 42, self-blame and guilt, p. 45 may be particularly useful to you, whilst "The grief experience" on p. 147 will give you some understanding of the mourning process.)

8. Bereavement through accidental drowning

I have deliberately included the word "accidental" in this title. Frequently when a young child drowns parents blame themselves for not having prevented it. They perceive the accident as tantamount to having committed murder. In the previous section I wrote about the fallibility of human beings. Somehow the fact of drowning seems to question the very gut of parents' sense of responsibility, their role as guardians and protectors.

Is it possible to be a mother or father who is never negligent, forgetful, careless? How many times have you and every other parent been in error without dire consequences? This once, what only happens to other people happened to you and you feel devastated as a result. Surely that is enough? What a high price to pay for not being there, or aware . . . The accident ended your child's life on earth, but would s/he wish you to continue to pay the terrible cost that self-accusation exacts from you? Is not the pain of loss ample penance? Do you have the right to play the part of punitive God? You block awareness of His compassion.

It is likely that you are haunted by the horror of finding your child, the panic during the resuscitation attempts, the imagining of what the experience must have been like for him/her. (When a drowning occurs

115

consciousness is lost quite quickly.) There is the urgent need to have a replay of the events and change the ending. Pools, associated with recreation, and baths or buckets have become threatening, lethal.

Perhaps your child drowned at sea and was not found, or only after some time. It is a nightmare and so difficult to prevent yourself from thoughts of his/her body and what might have happened to it. (See "When there is neither body nor ashes" on p. 120.) Whatever your child experienced is of no importance to him/her now. Talking over and over again about your fears, thoughts and feelings will free you of them.

A natural result of an accident is to become anxious and over-protective of the rest of your children. This need will settle as your courage for living gradually returns – and it will!

You may be deciding to move house. Although generally after a death you are well-advised not to make any major changes for the first year, when a child drowned at home remaining there may be just too painful. Try to desensitize yourself before making a major move you might later regret. If you cannot go near your pool, try to approach it gradually for a month or more, getting closer every few days. Make your own goals and set your own limits. You may need the support of an understanding and patient person during these attempts. Encouragement is a great help.

The sleep disturbances and physical and emotional distress will ease in time if you do not continue to punish yourself with self-blame for this death. Allow healing to take place.

9. The aftermath of suicide

Although it seems as if the sanctity of life has been violated there are two types of suicide; one is a negation, an escape from life. The other affirms it, in essence says: "There is more to living than this that I experience." The motive is to take control of what is unmanageable, accept the alternative to total defeat. It is a turning towards the light.

Today enlightened ministers of religion seem unanimous in their compassion and forgiveness once the act has been performed. Nevertheless, when a suicide occurred there are feelings (such as disgrace, rejection and personal negation) in family members that need to be worked through before normal grieving can begin. When it seems clear that your child chose suicide for life-affirming reasons you may not experience the same devastation that self-destruction usually brings in its wake. But this is not to say that your grief is not profound.

All the reactions shock, disbelief, denial and self-blame that accompany sudden, unexpected death are present when there was a suicide in the family. You question yourself, your spouse and children in the search for answers, and in the need to know that you (as a parent) have not failed absolutely. Even when the death was a turning towards the light, there is the anguish that life here seemed not worth living; that you were unable to make it worthwhile. There are some factors that cannot be offset. (See "Self-blame and guilt", p. 45.)

Grief reactions to suicide usually range back and forth through desolation, anger, bewilderment, bitterness, the search for reasons, powerlessness, fear of being driven insane and of never recovering from the shock. Physical symptoms of extreme stress are likely to be experienced along with nightmares. Some parents cannot cope with the fact of suicide and need to have the death termed "accidental", and some are spiritually agonised. The legalities and publicity increase the horror for those close to the deceased.

Perhaps more than after any other death family members are tortured by "if only's". These are fantasies that cannot be tested and found to be the truth. Try to let go of them. They will not bring you answers or peace of mind, but will lead you downward into despair and are habit-forming.

People grieve very differently and under the pressure that this death brings, the differences will be all the more marked. For this reason it is important that both of you have help in dealing with the loss if your marriage is not to become strained. Trauma can bring couples closer together, but far more commonly the stress separates. Sometimes parents remain together after a death because they must have someone to blame and so they remain locked with each other to meet this negative need. These issues will alert you to the wisdom of taking care of your relationship.

A marked difficulty for the family of someone who died by suicide is the lack of "rites of passage" after such a death. People seem not to know what to say or do and this adds to the sense of isolation that is associated with this loss. Religious sanctions against suicide, though far less strict today, may increase your feeling of being outcast. A sense of shame may weigh upon you.

Perhaps your child was on drugs, had been troubled for quite a while, depressed and/or a disruptive force in the family. However deep your love for him/her you may be relieved that release has come.

There are always many confused and mixed emotions after a death therefore it is understandable in these circumstances that you find consolation in family peace. There is still the grief. You may be feeling disloyal and unnatural if your pain is, in part, remedied. You do your child no dishonour by accepting your feelings. Indeed I have known a youngster who killed himself to free his loved ones from the torture he felt he could not help putting them through. His death was a gift of love, though it brought great anguish.

For his/her wellbeing you can affirm the value of the physical world by conscious appreciation of it. Give thought to the sanctity of the body, the wonder of creation. This will help to counterbalance the negation of material nature that the act of suicide has brought about.

10. The family and homicide

Because of the suddenness and violence of murder your equilibrium is overthrown. There is nothing that can prepare you for such outrage. Some of the horror is related to the fact that there was intent to kill. You may be tortured by the thought that perhaps it could have been prevented. Besides the fury and acute grief, the private hell that you are going through has to do with vulnerability and the violation of your child's very being. This is the terrible intrusiveness of homicide.

Many parents of murdered children maintain that their agony and fear are ignored or forgotten by society, and they feel isolated. Perhaps this is, in part, due to even those who wish to be of assistance feeling helpless and afraid in the face of this type of loss.

Because of the strong sense of unreality that accompanies an event such as homicide, it is advisable for parents and older children to see the body, even, if owing to disfigurement, just a hand can be left visible.

Information related to the manner of death helps you to believe that it has occurred. Usually there is a great need to know what happened; if not met, it can become obsessional. Only when the desired facts are provided is peace of mind possible.

You may be subject to mental visions of your child's last moments. Realise that shock anaesthetizes pain and so the suffering may well not have been at all as you are imagining.

Whilst some parents do not wish to know who committed the crime, others do. Some desire revenge. The need to retaliate is natural and understandable. The danger is that if you do not feel that the perpetrator is brought to justice your anger will in the end tend to consume you. There has been enough destruction already. The time must come when you allow anger to subside by relinquishing it without feeling disloyal.

In addition to the feelings of anger, fear and hatred towards the murderer you may, in you helplessness, be blaming yourself for not having been protective enough. Perhaps you are angry with your child for having been in the situation that led to the tragedy. Your family life is disrupted and you might experience a need for escape into alcohol, drugs and even suicide. It is not uncommon for paranoia to be experienced until some sense of personal security is regained. This is a period of your life so filled with nightmare that you would be wise to seek ongoing support for as long as you can benefit from it.

Investigations, the inquest and court hearings all keep the wound open and can keep you keyed up, anxiously awaiting further developments. It may seem as if your life will never again return to normal. Certainly it takes some time to do so, but working through your grief does gradually bring it back into focus. (See "Inquests", p. 64.)

Is there anything you can do against violent crime? Try to make contact with other parents bereaved in the same way and start campaigning for what you see as helpful both in prevention and after-care of survivors. Positive action is valuable and an effective means of self-rehabilitation.

Meaninglessness is one of the most difficult things to deal with. It questions religious, spiritual and philosophical convictions, undermining the security of beliefs. For this reason maybe murder should be viewed in isolation, as outside normality, segregated from faith and the values by which you live.

But in terms of your not being outside your own value system I want to say to those of you who are some years beyond your loss and are past all the inquiries and any trials that may have been held, it would be healing for you to go beyond the outrage. By continuing to harbour vengeance, to whatever degree, you perpetrate the violence. You do your child no honour thereby. Moving through your emotions to acceptance and ultimately to forgiveness will bring you the balm of longed- for consolation. (You might find the section on setting goals, p. 51 helpful.)

11. When there is neither body nor ashes

The psychological value of viewing a body, attending a funeral or cremation lies in bringing home to the mourners the fact of the death. Without recognition of it, grieving cannot proceed. Saying goodbye has reality when a body or ashes are present.

It is much more difficult for you to confront and dispel the illusion that your child is still alive in the absence of material proof of his/her death. Disbelief, which always follows news of an unexpected loss, has no proof of finality to offset it. Whilst a memorial service is a help and a comfort (even more so when it is personalised and even taped for re-living to help you grasp the reality), having no opportunity to make chosen arrangements for laying the body to rest deprives you of your last offering to a loved child.

In a situation where there are no remains there are many unanswered questions that can ensnare you and interfere with the grief process. Some can be dealt with, whilst others can perhaps be set aside by recognising that they are unanswerable now and that in the fullness of time you will gain understanding.

The body is precious; we relate to one another in physical form. A personal searching for your son/daughter may go on for a long time and be evident in a number of ways such as listening for his/her return, scanning faces in a crowd, watching the mail, wandering about without quite knowing why.

With nothing other than absence, and with the desire to resist acknowledging the truth, finality is hard for you to accept.

You may feel the need for a grave or garden of remembrance to visit: a place to which you can bring flowers, where you can sit for a while and be in communion with your child. It may be helpful for you to realise that s/he is with you wherever you are, whatever happened to the body. For those who could go to a local garden of remembrance, spending time there may be comforting – for it is just that: a place of remembrance.

Because it is so hard to accept the death as a fact it might become difficult if not almost impossible to dispose of your child's personal belongings. Under normal circumstances this takes a while, but here you are dealing with the daytime fantasy and nightly dreams that s/he will return. In the absence of body or ashes to authenticate the death, it may seem disloyal, a betrayal, to give away clothes or toys. The unreality of the loss is a strong and complicating factor.

Pay close attention to whatever written communication or other material proof of loss you have. However painful, it is necessary to your progress towards healing. Because you are tortured by the hell of uncertainty you may find that though at times you hold fast to it because of the chance of return, at other times you actually want proof of the death to release you from futile hopes. This may bring feelings of self-censure in its wake, as though you are wishing your child dead. All you are wanting is the truth.

Information regarding the circumstances of the death is relevant to your recovery, not only in terms of the loss becoming factual but to offset any trouble you may be having with fantasies about the fate of the body. For instance if your child died in a fire or at sea and you have nightmares about burning or drowning, know that whatever happened the shock anaesthetized pain and none of it matters to your son/daughter anymore. Material issues are of no relevance in the spiritual realm.

When the Helderberg went down I encouraged mourners to consider the cleanness, quiet and peace of the ocean depths rather than imagine shark damage (as some did).

As Westerners we need to have reasons for events in our lives. If the death of your child seems meaningless, you can in time give significance and purpose to it, perhaps by helping others in the same situation, by teaching compassion as your understanding grows or by any other means that you find appropriate.

12. Social unrest, terrorism, military and police action, judicial execution

Because there are so many facets I will focus mainly on common responses to them, as you may derive some consolation from finding you are not alone and that your reactions are normal.

Where you stand ideologically makes a great difference to the meaning the death has for you. If you are committed to the struggle it may have some relevance, because you can then allow yourself the mixed pride and grief that are natural after the death of a child.

If you feel that you have fed the beliefs or anger that have resulted in a death, whether your child's or even caused by him, you might be mourning him/her or the deed with heavy self-condemnation.

If s/he is seen as hero(ine) or martyr and becomes a public figure, your privacy is infringed upon. It might be difficult for you to grieve personally for your child as s/he 'belongs' to everyone.

On the other hand, if news of the loss of your child is met with public satisfaction, grief and anger may be mixed with shame. Public opinion may view the death as appropriate punishment; something that will be incredibly hard for you to bear and live with.

When death occurs as a public spectacle the horror is compounded by the exposure of something so personal as individual dying.

The opposite of this is the news of loss after a period of disappearance. Because anticipation of death by unnatural means is psychologically stressful, your fearing and expecting it would have left you emotionally undermined by the time you knew the outcome. You may experience a sense of relief after a period of uncertainty. This may cause a feeling of guilt, but your relief is natural. Anger and desperation in both cases are serious issues: they undermine psychological health when they are not appropriately recognised and worked through.

When you fear authority, brutality or reprisals, grief may be suppressed and this is at cost. Bans on funerals and mourning also complicate the grieving process.

Feeling immobilised, impotent or passive in the face of death caused by social unrest can lead to or be the result of depression.

The outrage that you experience when your child died as an innocent victim of a bomb in a public place is coupled with the shock of so violent and unexpected a death. There may have been severe mutilation and this adds to the revulsion and psychological trauma. Survivor guilt might plague you. (See p. 45 about self-blame and guilt and p. 42 about anger.)

The expression of your grief is all-important. Find release for it in any way that you can, for held in it gains weight.

13. Multiple losses: simultaneous and sequential

There is some overlap in these two situations so whilst I have divided the sections for clarity, it does form one whole.

● *Simultaneous deaths*

When the deaths of two or more members of the family occur concurrently, the sense of loss is compounded much beyond that which might seem proportional. In other words the loss of two children does not bring twice the grief but far more than that. Added to the anguish is an overwhelming feeling of vulnerability.

Response to such deprivation depends upon how many survivors there are in the family and how meaningful the remaining relationships are. The number and significance of the deceased, and the cause of death are also relevant.

The initial shock of witnessing or hearing of the simultaneous death of your loved ones may have temporarily deranged you. For quite some time you might have had to block out realisation of the facts because they were too threatening even to countenance. Perhaps you resisted having anyone talk of the deaths. How fearsome it is to gradually allow the truth to sink in. Maybe you needed to take tranquillizers to tide you over the first period as the shock wore off.

Burial, cremation or a memorial service with more than one coffin is traumatic but valuable. Prior denial of loss can then no longer be complete and the normal grief process can begin.

You are likely to feel that your situation is unreal, completely insecure and lonely; even if you have a spouse and other surviving children. You have had varied relationships with different family members and grieving for more than one at a time can be emotionally complicated. The differing interactions that you had may now manifest as a confusion of loyalties (one closer: another less close?), which could lead to some remorse if there was any favouritism in the family. Your anguish will be profound and the outraged questions: "Why me?", "Why us?", "Why them?" might be asked for a long time.

When multiple tragedies occur survivor guilt tends to be strong. It is most important to have professional help both for you and your family after a great and complex loss. Trauma can be so dislocating that support becomes essential.

● *Sequential deaths*
The length of the time lapse(s) between the deaths have a significant bearing upon your ability to deal effectively with your bereavement. As with simultaneous deaths, the family remaining and your particular relationship with those who died affect your grieving. How have you coped with previous losses? Have you been able to complete your mourning? You may find yourself dealing with residues of past grief now.

Perhaps you feel depleted, drained of the energy to start all over again.

Loss does not get easier to bear. Having experienced death in your family you know that the path is long and difficult. You need encouragement as it is difficult to believe in your own ongoing resilience. And yet no burden is too heavy; it is up to you to use the strength and coping skills provided.

● *Multiple losses*

Depression is part of the mourning process. After multiple losses it is likely that you will need some help to become sufficiently energised to deal with your grief-work. In this context anti-depressants may be of value. A doctor who understands mourning will be able to give you appropriate advice.

Expression of grief is the path to healing, but with many or repeated losses you may think that you cannot go on expecting people to listen and to hold you whilst you cry.

Writing becomes a valuable way of dealing with your pain. You might keep a journal: First list the feelings you are experiencing. Then take them one by one and write about them. For instance, describe the anger, and the recent incidents when you felt irritable, annoyed, enraged . . . "Mary always scolds her poor kids: she should know how lucky she is to have any children at all. I can't bear hearing her." Continuing for a while releases a fair amount of pain and is therefore restorative.

You may prefer to (repeatedly) tell the story of your losses, or pour your grief out in poems or letters. Even if no-one ever reads them they will have a therapeutic effect.

The question of immortality might be troubling you. Your children carry on the family name, the family line. Losing them prior to their having had children of their own leaves you with a lessened future. Yet immortality takes many forms: amongst others, the continuance of the spirit after death and the eternal aspect of nature and our oneness with it. If you believe that in reality there is no essential separateness you will see that in the larger sense immortality is not denied you.

Because multiple loss is so extreme a situation you are well-advised to pay special attention to your well-being. Accept help offered by others and do not allow yourself to skimp on self-care. You may feel that life is not worth living and there is no meaning in it anymore. Take the decision to keep going, make contact with The Compassionate Friends, see a counsellor, therapist or minister. Your feelings are understandable, natural – but in the months that lie ahead your desperation will change. Gradually recovery will begin. Choose to live, and live to choose healing.

II
Sibling's grief

1. How do I tell the children?

Adults sometimes think that small children are too young to know anything about death. Yet they have observed that flowers and beetles die, have seen a dead bird in the road and have possibly already lost a pet. So even if the loss of a sibling is their first encounter with a human death, the subject is not entirely new to them.

When a death occurs in a family even the youngest of children knows something is wrong and is upset if excluded from sharing the grief. It is scary for a child to hear or witness crying and not have any explanation, and disturbing to perceive the veiled emotion that is so apparent to his concerned eyes.

Telling a child about the demise of a sibling is made easier if the age and stage of understanding is taken into account. When being told bad news he needs loving encompassment – to be held, allowed to cry or scream out, encouraged to express thoughts, fears, questions; given time to think and the liberty to return to the subject when he needs to.

Children's reactions can be unexpected. If shortly after being told of a sibling's death your son/daughter seems to be playing unconcernedly, laughing or becoming over-excited, it may be because the loss is not perceived as final – its meaning has not been absorbed. Anxiety might be denied, and the tension felt is discharged in activity. Do not get offended or angry: he does not know how to deal with emotions and stress. Children need help to mourn.

● *The stages of understanding death*
☐ The *infant* is responsive to separation from what he needs, though he has not yet defined himself as distinct from any other person.

☐ As the *baby* learns to distinguish between individuals he becomes anxious if those important to him do not reappear.

☐ It is well-known that *toddlers* experience separation anxiety though there is, as yet, no concept of time.

127

☐ A *child above the age of two* can achieve a basic understanding of "dead" if helped to do so. There is a matter-of-fact curiosity about death at this stage. Clear simple and realistic information is best, with support for the feelings evoked.

☐ *Up to five years* children regard death as akin to sleep: impermanent and reversible. You are dead and you wake up again. So as not to cause further confusion do not use terms such as "gone to sleep" or "gone away" when referring to death.

They think in concrete terms and are interested in body functions and causes of death. They probably hold a number of conflicting views and therefore some of the questions asked will be muddled: e.g. "How will Janey get out of the box when she is dead?"

They tend to equate death with killing and can become very afraid of the perceived potency of aggression. Cause and effect are taken literally: if your child has thought or said that he wished a sibling was dead or would go away and not come back (and which child has not?), he feels responsible when the sib dies. It is of paramount importance to tell children that they have not caused the death and to give the actual reason for it in terms they can understand. (Where death has been by suicide I do not believe it appropriate to explain it to a young child. I prefer to use the word "accident" and give the accurate explanations that are necessary when the child is much older.)

☐ The *five to eight year old* believes that death comes from an external source (e.g. a bogeyman) that might be outwitted or conquered. Some children in this age group recognise that it is a permanent state. There is great interest in burial rites, as shown by the elaborate funerals that pets are given.

☐ By *eight or nine* death is feared, because it is seen as irreversible, and as happening to anyone (even to the child himself). Though understood to be caused by natural processes there may yet be subconscious anxiety that something he did led to the sibling's loss of life. It is natural to regress to an earlier stage under stress. Thus reassurance must be given.

☐ From *nine to twelve* abstract thought is developing and there may be interest in a spiritual world. The consequences of death are of concern: e.g. "What will we do now?".

In summary: With sensitivity, awareness and honesty use language appropriate to your child's level of understanding and avoid inaccuracies or euphemisms – e.g. "Danny went on a long journey", "We lost our child", "God picks the prettiest flowers". Reassure your child that whilst God does not take children, He does receive them.

Accept that your youngsters will not react just as you do. Observe them, and allow them to express feelings, thoughts and questions. Be accepting, loving, comforting, and reassuring. If you feel unable to cope with your children owing to your own grief, ask someone trustworthy to help you. Do not send them away; they need to be part of the family experience. Their fantasies of what is going on when they are not there, are far worse than the reality.

Finally, a clarification of death that Elisabeth Kubler-Ross uses with young children involves an analogy between the emergence of the butterfly from the chrysalis and the spirit or soul's freedom to leave the body when it has no further use for it.

2. The needs of young children

Integration and disintegration are part of the rhythm of life's cycle and even young children are aware of them. Their response to death depends upon the experiences they have had (dead plants, caterpillars, birds, etc.) and the reactions of the people around them. Protecting children by keeping reality hidden isolates them and cheats them of the opportunity to learn how to deal with grief.

Because a child is often afraid of and does not know what to do with strong emotions, he needs to be reassured that they are normal and acceptable. He must know that it is good to be honest with feelings and thoughts. The child requires to be taught how to express them and that though people cry when sad, they are consolable. The pain of loss eases with time just as a sore tummy gets better; sadness is another kind of hurting.

Do not be afraid to shed tears in front of him. In telling your son that big boys do not cry you are encouraging him to grow up with a limited capacity for emotional expression and little healthy outlet for his feelings. Children need to know what their family members are experiencing. They test their own responses against those of adults. By example you can teach your child not to bottle emotions and how to express them without doing any damage. A great deal can be worked through in play.

The difference between thoughts, words and actions should be explained because young children believe that wishing someone dead can kill him. Feelings are not good or bad; it is what is done with them and the actions they prompt that are good or bad, appropriate or not.

It often happens that just when his needs are greatest your own grief is depleting you of the resources to help him effectively. This is the time to ask someone you trust and who understands your child to help him – truthfully and with tact. He may find it easier to speak to someone outside the family circle, perhaps to protect you. I have worked with little ones as young as four years of age who felt a need to shield their parents.

Your child's loss must be acknowledged, not only by the immediate family but also by friends, teachers (who should be informed of the death in the family), the minister, and others who come into contact with him. Without this recognition his mourning is inhibited.

His grief and the timing thereof is unique and different to yours because his relationship with the deceased child was not the same. The children have laughed and fought together, confided and played and one must now face going on without the other.

He may regret the mean things said or done and find it difficult to forgive himself. He may be scared by the intensity of the pain he experiences and is probably hurting on your behalf as well. He wants things to be the same as before, yet finds it hard to believe that they ever will. He might also be feeling different to his playmates and uncomfortable about that.

The bereaved child is impatient for attention because he feels insecure and helpless. Hold him close with the assurance that his life will return to normal.

If death has come after illness he may feel relieved that the suffering is over and that now he can be paid more attention. He might reproach himself for this, though these feelings are quite natural.

Guilt can plague youngsters and they should be encouraged to discuss it. They can be comforted by remembering all the positive aspects of their relationship with their sibling. Maybe the anger at what has happened to their sib and all the family is difficult to deal with and get rid of. It may be directed at you or at God for not preventing the death, and/or at the brother/sister for dying and causing all this trouble and sadness.

Survivor guilt can trouble children and sometimes a child may think that his parents would have preferred to have the deceased sib back and him dead instead. This can be a reaction to the extreme grief observed. Once again, loving reassurance is essential.

Communication is vital. Some children are articulate, ask questions and explain how they see and feel about things whereas others tend to be quiet and need gentle drawing out. Often an adult has to help them by verbalising what they might be experiencing.

Listen to his questions and comments; ask him for clarification. Often adults think youngsters comprehend what they are being told but the child's understanding might be quite different. If the sibling died of an illness, name it so that the next time your surviving child is unwell he does not think he will die.

Withhold the information you feel will be overwhelming and do not be afraid to say that you have no answers to some questions, if that is the truth. Avoid saying anything you may need to contradict later on.

Children, like adults, need to say goodbye. If he was too young or did not want to attend the funeral, there are ways of bidding farewell that will help him to accept the reality of the death and close the chapter on that part of his sibling's life. Goodbyes can be verbalised, written down or acted out with playthings. A "goodbye picture" can be drawn. Perhaps a visit to the cemetery or a garden of remembrance is appropriate, but should be with someone who will not become distraught and only after an explanation of what it will be like.

If the death of the sib leaves your youngster an only child or particularly lonely he might invent an imaginary playmate to fill the gap. Usually this fantasy friend fades out in time and should not cause undue concern.

Keeping the deceased child's room and all belongings exactly as they were when s/he died can anger the surviving one because so much is invested in the child who is no longer there. Your surviving child is likely to perceive this as being at his expense. Shrining, which involves some idealisation of the dead, represents a denial of reality which is confusing. Your child may react with anxiety and regressive behaviour to get attention and reassurance.

He should be allowed to distract himself with activities when necessary, have keepsakes of his sibling's and have the freedom to visit or not visit the grave. Children generally know what they need even if unable to verbalise it.

You may find that he takes on some of his dead sib's characteristics for a while – e.g.: a lisp, a style of walking or even the type of pain the brother/sister was experiencing. This is a way of trying to hold on to

131

the departed child and should be allowed – though physical pain should be investigated to be sure that there is nothing organically wrong.

Sleep and eating disturbances are common during the mourning period. You might want to leave a night-light burning; serve small portions of appetizing, nutritious food and if your child is compensating for his loss by overeating, offer hugs in place of the second helping. Sometimes when older children cook, their eating difficulty evens out.

The brother/sister who died lives on in the memories the family have of him/her. If you believe in life after death you will be explaining that to your child. A way to define spirit for a youngster is to describe it as the part of each person that cannot be touched. You feel happy yet cannot hold happiness; you know you are loved but love cannot be physically clasped.

If your child tells you that he feels the presence of, or has seen the deceased sibling, do not dismiss this experience. If he is afraid, give the reassurance that no harm is meant; it is just a visit and he is blessed.

Your child needs to be told that he is special and a real consolation. Encourage him in all his abilities, to increase his confidence during this time of confusion and uncertainty. Allow his feelings to take precedence over the activities that you can set aside so that you are available to listen and to give him comfort and support.

3. Children and funerals

The grief of children is often unrecognised, dismissed, ignored or misunderstood. Bereaved parents may be so bereft that they simply are not available to help them understand and cope with their feelings. (I suggest that you read the two sections, "How do I tell the children" on p. 127, and "The needs of young children" on p. 129, first.)

Children can be encouraged to see their sibling after death if there is someone available and close enough to explain to them that the body will be (getting) cold. Allow them to touch or not, as they wish. Viewing does make the death a reality, and this is helpful. It takes care of many of the frightening fantasies.

If your child died at home, that is the best place for the remaining children to spend some time with him/her. If the viewing will be at a funeral parlour or in church your children need to be prepared for the experience.

Where mutilation has been severe it may well be advisable for the surviving siblings not to be exposed to that. Perhaps a hand can be seen and held – but once again, appropriate explanations must be offered so that they feel more secure and their imaginations do not run wild.

Whether they should be included at funeral ceremonies depends upon your views, their ages and what they prefer. No unwilling child should be made to participate or feel guilty about not doing so. If a child of five years or older very much wants to be included he should be; if the service becomes too much for him, he can be taken out. Excluding him when he wishes to attend, isolates him and leaves him with fantasies that might be very troublesome. The memorial service, funeral or cremation is an opportunity to bid his sibling goodbye, and to be rightfully included as a member of the grieving family.

It is helpful to the child if the rites, who will attend, who will sit next to him and what will take place, are explained beforehand. Advice on how to reply when people condole with him is valuable. He should be given the opportunity to express his feelings and be encouraged to ask questions. An adult who will not be overwhelmed with grief should take care of him, hold his hand, and take him onto his/her lap if necessary. Physical contact is consoling and gives a sense of security. Sometimes a child is much comforted by having a toy or a letter he has written or drawn put into the coffin.

A child older than seven can be encouraged to attend. Children need to participate in family events. They can assist in planning the funeral, be given tasks such as handing out programmes and helping to serve tea afterwards. I have met many youngsters who have deeply regretted being excluded at a time when they needed solace, to be of comfort and part of the ceremony for a loved family member.

Children often feel overlooked and crowded out at the gathering after the funeral. They are anxious to have life return to normal once more. Again, special care needs to be taken to ensure their well-being.

Having read these general guidelines, take the decisions with your family that you feel are in your children's best interests. You know their temperaments, how mature they are and how sensitive. Even if you decide they should not attend the funeral do include them as much as possible. Generally speaking, if adults can hold steady the children can too.

4. Explaining cremation to young children

I am often asked how cremation can be explained to young children. To do so, first consider a number of factors:

Up to the age of about seven years children assume that others think and feel as they do. They tend to endow inanimate objects with human characteristics; an example is the hurt child's retaliatory kick at the "naughty chair" he has just fallen off. So the dead are generally thought of as alive and responsive.

Also remember that the less a child is able to understand the meaning of death (i.e. the younger he is) the more he relies upon the atmosphere that surrounds the events – the way in which the adults are responding – and the more likely it is that he will misinterpret it.

Because the young child is so literal in his thinking (abstract thought cannot be expected until about nine to twelve years of age), great care must be taken in the words chosen for explanations. It is always useful to both adult and child if careful questioning can elicit what his understanding is of what he is being told. So often we assume that we have made ourselves clear, only to be amazed at the child's interpretation! Sally, aged five, had heard that all souls go to heaven. When asked what she thought it was like there she said that there had to be rows and rows of shelves with shoes laid side by side upon them. She understood "souls" to be "soles".

Although the above example is amusing, children have vivid imaginations and can create frightening images which may be more difficult for them to deal with than the reality appropriately presented. Their fantasies can interfere with sleep, and induce nightmares as well as daytime fears.

Anxiety about death-related issues and a consequent need to protect your children can interfere with your ability to communicate naturally with them. Children are able to cope admirably with any facts presented in a tone of voice and way which convey love, caring and an honest attempt to include them, help them understand, and be of comfort. You may well be feeling upset and insecure; it is alright to say so. Explain that the family is very sad and can cry together and share thoughts, questions and feelings. There are things that cannot always be understood, but it helps to talk about them. Because children are sensitive to underlying emotions in those close to them, ideally discussions and explanations should take place when you are feeling inwardly steady and able to manage.

When explaining cremation (I am not advocating it rather than burial; my intent is only to clarify it for the child) keep the above factors in mind. Whatever explanation you feel is appropriate for your children, offer it reassuringly, hold them close, and go slowly, giving them time to ask questions or make comments.

I deal here with the physical aspects of cremation and not the spiritual, for this depends so much upon the family's religious or philosophical orientation. Nevertheless I tackle the whole subject from the standpoint of death as relating to the body only, the spirit being eternal. What I have outlined above will, I trust, help you to give explanations that suit your beliefs, deal with other issues that you may wish to consider, and with the questions you may be asked.

The following example is a guide and not a blueprint. I call the child who died, Tommy.

"Tommy is dead and that means that he does not feel things like you and I do, anymore. He doesn't feel hot or cold, or that he is hurting, or cross, or hungry. Because his body is dead he cannot live in it any longer. It is a bit like the butterfly coming out of its chrysalis, that brown covering that it does not need when it is ready to fly away in the sunlight.

"There are two things we can do with Tommy's body, and we must choose one of them because we cannot keep it. You know that when animals and birds die their bodies soon change and start to decay (like the leaves in the garden that make good compost when they are dead). That happens to dead people too: so we must decide what we want to do now.

"We can put Tommy's body in a special box called a coffin and bury it in the ground in a place called a cemetery, where lots of other people's bodies are also buried. Or we can take it to another place where it will be put in a very small room (not like any we have in our home). All that is in it is a very hot fire which changes the body into ashes, and that is called cremation. Don't forget that Tommy cannot feel anymore because his body is dead and he is like the butterfly that has flown away. That part of Tommy we call his spirit. When we want to, we can take the ashes and bury them in the ground or we can scatter them in a place that we choose."

Whatever modifications you wish to make to this sample explanation (if you wish to use it at all) will be appropriate for you and your children if they make you feel more comfortable. Omit any parts that you feel are superfluous; I have made it detailed to cover all aspects. Whatever you intend to do with the ashes can be substituted for the two options given above. Reassure your children that their deceased brother or sister will always be loved and remembered even though s/he is no longer physically here.

Children love ceremonies; if you feel they could be included in whatever is planned for the disposal of the ashes, give them the option to attend. First explain what will take place and who will be there. Make sure that someone will be present who can take care of them if you may be too distressed to do so.

It is comforting to cry together, but if you feel that explanations relating to the loss are too overwhelming, they can be undertaken by someone else whom you can trust to deal appropriately with them for you.

5. The bereaved adolescent

For adolescents death is an abstract concept, is feared, and is distant. These views are reinforced by the immediacy of their concerns and the growth and development of their bodies. They are at a stage when they are seeking identity and greater independence, testing concepts, and looking towards the future. At the same time they are being swung about emotionally by hormonal changes.

In a sense the adolescent is in a marginal situation: no longer a child and not yet adult. He is in transit between the two and this causes tension, much seeking and questioning. There are so few signposts to show the way in a fast changing world of insecure adults.

Teenagers require a great deal of emotional support and the opportunity to express their grief and their concerns. The death of a sibling brings an enormous amount of anxiety and places huge demands upon youngsters in this age group. Every aspect of their lives is affected just when they feel unsure of both themselves and their coping abilities.

People regress when under stress. The teenager is just becoming less dependent when loss arouses in him the needs of a child – to be held, comforted, made to feel secure – and he vacillates between struggling against them to assert his maturity, and giving in.

Adolescence is also a time of testing relationship skills and finding new ways of interacting with others. The death of a brother or sister, bringing in its wake as it does all the confused feelings and outraged thoughts of grief, seems to undermine growing confidence. Closeness often appears threatening in the face of loss.

The relationship with the deceased sibling is likely to have been changeable to some extent, and this leaves the surviving sib with self-accusation and possibly anger towards his brother/sister. This in turn can evoke feelings of guilt and with the intensity of adolescence it is a depleting and exhausting process. (Being angry does restore some of the sense of power lost in the feelings of helplessness and yearning.)

Some other experiences that teenagers have after the death of a sibling are great loneliness, loss of childhood, having been cheated out of a brother/sister and a strong sense of the unfairness of it. There may be a pervasive sense of inadequacy to deal with all they are confronted with. There is often a turning against, if not away from, God.

The need to talk about the loss may be strong and is often thwarted by peer group members' unwillingness to listen. People generally seem to show concern only for the parents. There is the expectation of some that the adolescent will get over his grief in a matter of weeks. All this causes mounting frustration if not anger.

On the positive side, teenagers are generally more able to cope with the immediate impact of circumstances than younger children. They are better able to work through some of their grief by caring for family members and recalling times with the deceased sib. Their health is usually not impaired as is that of adults, though depression is not uncommon.

You can help your teenage children by talking openly (though not too repetitively) about your deceased child and by really listening to what they want to say. They need to regain and increase their shaken sense of confidence and you can assist them by affirming your love and appreciation of them and of anything positive they do. Hugs and holding are reassuring and give a sense of much-needed security.

Show them respect for their way of grieving as distinct from yours. They need to know they can be themselves – though you do not have to be afraid of setting limits when necessary. Appropriate discipline assures your children that you care.

Encourage the development of outside relationships and show interest in them, fostering the resilience typical of youth. Expectations of academic achievement must be modified for quite some time. Concentration is difficult and motivation is lessened. Ask your teenagers to do the best they can.

As family members they need to be included in the plans, rites and ceremonies that accompany the death. The first viewing can be a shock to an adolescent. His reactions may help him to release any suppressed feelings of guilt he might have. Death, particularly of someone in the same age group, brings him face to face with his own mortality and this is very disturbing to the young. He will require much support and understanding as he struggles to come to terms with death itself, and the loss of his sib.

The section that follows deals further with parent/adolescent interaction. You may feel unable at present to offer much to your children. Nevertheless it is always possible to make some effort to restore balance in the family, and teenagers are able to do their part. Mutual concern for the well-being of the group can do wonders and be most encouraging.

6. Bereaved teenage and adult siblings in relation to their parents

My intention here is to meet the need expressed by bereaved parents to understand their teenagers. I hope to assist the latter as well.

In addition to siblings' pain and their multi-faceted sense of loss and anxiety at facing their own mortality, there is the difficulty of feeling different to their peers. Added to their anger, sense of guilt and of the irreversibility of the death, is their distress in relation to your grief.

● *What parents need to understand about the feelings of their children*
☐ You may be inconsolable for a time and it is:
  ☐ painful for them to witness anguish in loved ones;
  ☐ difficult to live with, partly because they seem to have lost relevance and feel helpless;
  ☐ frightening because it seems as if life will never again be relaxed and happy.

☐ It is scary not knowing what is normal, in grieving. Not understanding that it is alright to laugh and to forget for a while can lead to feelings of anxiety and guilt.

☐ The death in the family affects concentration and so studies may suffer. Youngsters need understanding and revised expectations of their standard of work.

138

☐ Surviving children (whether teenage or adult) may feel they have to compensate for their parents' loss – be two people and not just themselves. Because this is not possible, it is a heavy burden. Survivor guilt contributes to attempts to recompense, and is hard for them to bear.

☐ Youngsters and adults protect their parents and shoulder their responsibilities which delay their mourning. Much later they may have to grieve alone because for others the worst is over and they have moved on ahead.

☐ Support for siblings is usually minimal. Family and friends are concerned about the parents. Perhaps they have no idea what to say to the siblings.

☐ Communication, often problematic in families at the best of times, can become a huge issue after a sibling's death. Conversation may seem impossible, become highly emotional and therefore be avoided. It might sometimes be misunderstood, accusatory and hurtful. Anger can become destructive or manipulative on both sides. Grief can play havoc with relationships unless reasonable limits are set.

☐ Many children try their best to help, to keep the peace, avoid upsets and be supportive . . . often without any success. This is not because you do not want the same things – stability, comfort, etc. – but because you are all so torn, vulnerable and possibly struggling with blame and self-accusation.

☐ Some teenagers feel they can never "get it right". If they cry they upset their families, and if they do not they might be regarded as uncaring. There is a sense of desperation when nothing seems to go well. Perhaps parents feel that way too.

☐ Parental over-protectiveness (initially a very natural reaction) can be difficult for both teenagers and adults, particularly at a time when they are moving or have moved away from childhood dependency.

☐ A sense of loyalty and anxiety concerning you may make it very hard for the child or children still living at home to leave, whether on holiday, to study, or to move out. You most likely do not want to curtail freedom, yet may have great difficulty in letting another child go. After a loss, separation can seem like another death until equilibrium and perspective are restored.

☐ Perhaps death came at a time when your teenagers were trying to sort out meanings in relation to morality, ideological and spiritual standpoints. The death of a young person seems to reverse the natural order and can cause confusion, fear and a sense of meaninglessness.

☐ Some categories of death pose more of a threat than others (e.g. suicide, violence, murder). Fear and insecurity are more pervasive after a sudden traumatic death. Your children probably feel they must reassure you as to the quality of your parenting if a suicide has taken place.

☐ The child who died was no saint! Surviving youngsters feel undervalued by comparison when their brother/sister is idealised. If the deceased receives most attention, insecurity and anger may compound the surviving children's grief.

☐ Siblings often know one another better than you do, so their loss has a particular intensity and specificity. It must be expressed and shared.

☐ Youngsters may watch your marriage become strained and feel anxious, perhaps blame you, whilst feeling helpless.

☐ Those sibs who are themselves adults and have children of their own, may fear for their safety and in turn overprotect them.

☐ They may find their family life greatly disrupted by the concern and care they offer you.

● *What parents can do to help their children*
Some of the keys to resolving loss-related family issues are: loving understanding, care in communication, patience, respect for yourself, your children and the grief process.

☐ Show your teenagers and adult children that they are important; be aware and reassuring that recovery will come to all of you. Let your grieving be a model for theirs: accept your varied emotions as a natural part of mourning and find appropriate ways of expressing them. It is alright, indeed healthy for both men and women to cry.

☐ Answer their questions as best you can, admit to your confusion and share time talking, listening and hugging. Be aware that though their grief is different to yours, it too is deep, and frightening at times. Grief work is hard work: there is no other effective way.

☐ Recognise that for a time your children have not only lost a brother or sister but their parents as well. Be kind and gentle to yourself, and with them.

☐ Relax whilst trying to improve communication; there is a time for speaking and a time for silence – both must be respected. Explaining how you feel may help if it leads to understanding and greater closeness. You might disagree with your children's sentiments or viewpoints, but accept their feelings and their individuality.

☐ Your remaining children are different to the one who died: relate to them as they are. Whilst pining for your deceased child it is so easy to want his/her role in your life filled by one of the others. Unwittingly expectations can be placed that should not be met because each child is a unique gift, special as him/herself.

☐ Take care of your marriage. It is under a great deal of strain during bereavement and needs patience, love and flexibility.

☐ Create times as a family for relief of grief – a braai, a film evening – whatever you can all escape into together. It may help to include a few friends.

☐ Bear in mind that if your youngsters are adolescents, in addition to coping with their own grief and that of those they love, they are going through all the turbulence of normal developmental changes and tensions.

☐ Try not to blame yourself, your spouse or children for the disorder of your family life at present. Accusation and judgement cannot achieve positive goals. Rather share the responsibility for resolving it.

A round-the-table meeting once a week has been found useful. Each person has an opportunity to share his thoughts, experiences and feelings and to report and affirm his own progress (e.g. "I could go into Danny's room without crying this week"). Acknowlegement is also made of other members' progress.

☐ Recognise and discuss your tendency to over-protect. It stems from both love and fear. You know that youngsters cannot be kept at home or have activities too strictly curtailed. Risks are part of living and if "safe" must be taken. Your confidence will return as time passes with no further loss. Perhaps a mutually agreed upon contract between you and your children will make you feel safer and allow them some leeway.

☐ TCF meetings are most helpful. Sharing common experiences, you find you are not alone and you are normal. There is nothing like diving in and taking a restorative swim in a supportive pool! If you feel you are not coping with your pain and family tensions, seek help from a counsellor, therapist or minister who understands grief. Do not assume that family dissention will just "blow over". Rather make sure that you are all taken care of during this most vulnerable time.

● *A special word to grieving siblings*
Possibly your greatest need is to understand what mourning is all about, and that your feelings (however way-out and scary they seem) are normal. Knowing that your parents will come through their grief too and that life will settle down again, is reassuring. Is there someone understanding and available with whom you can talk, cry, be angry and feel scared? Perhaps at the moment what you want is more privacy: can you ask your family for that?

At times you may need to get out and away from all the anguish whilst at other times you might feel safer at home. All these feelings and many, many more are natural; you are not going crazy.

Are you preoccupied with a sense of guilt in relation to your sib for things you think you should or should not have done . . .? Are you distressed at being alive when s/he is dead and does that make you feel that you have no right to enjoy life?

● *How to handle difficult issues*
☐ Read the sections about grief so that you understand what you are

dealing with and what is happening to you and your parents. TCF newsletters are useful too. An excellent publication is *The courage to grieve* (see the list at the end of this book), while *The bereaved parent* has an excellent chapter for siblings.

☐ A person or group to share your feelings with, and from whom you can get perspective and support, can usefully supplement family discussion.

☐ Your increasing understanding of what is involved in coping with grief, will provide a basis from which you can begin to use your insight and have more meaningful and productive interactions with your parents. You will begin to feel less helpless.

☐ Try to improve communication with your family members. Enlist their help for mutual benefit. Fears, worries, and anger can be allayed when shared. There is a time for protectiveness and a time for talking openly together.

☐ Co-operate with, or help your parents to find solutions to their need to over-protect you. They, like you, are shaken and insecure.

☐ No-one is ever given more to bear than he is able to. It is up to you to choose to work through your pain in all the ways outlined here. However afraid you are of the intensity of your feelings, you are not going to go crazy.

☐ The feeling that you have no right to an enjoyable life anymore is one that your parents may share. Your sibling would surely not want you to miss out on the good times. If you had died and s/he survived would you want him/her to grieve forever and have no more joy or fun, achievements or new discoveries? Surely not: so accept that you have the right to go on fully living your life – even if at the moment you do not want to. In time you will become enthusiastic again and that is worth waiting for and working towards.

☐ Often bereaved people feel suicidal, but the wish to die passes. If you feel this way, talk to someone you can trust and who can help you. It will be a great relief.

☐ What were your strong points before your sister/brother died? You may feel you have lost touch with any talents you had, as if all has changed. Things have altered and no-one will be quite the same as before, but that does not mean you have lost everything or will not all recover. What you were, you are still. List your strengths and special abilities and see how they can be put to use, however hard it is at first. You will get in touch with your old self and find that you have choices. You are not just a victim of your loss and your feelings.

☐ Be yourself. Offer comfort and support to your parents but do not try to be the sib that died. There are two reasons for my saying this:
  ☐ You are special and can only find fulfilment in life by being who you really are.
  ☐ Trying to be someone else does not work. It negates who you are and you end up feeling lonely and frustrated. You will become angry with your sib and that will lead to feelings of great discomfort.

☐ Even though right now the world seems a senseless, unfair place and life has little value, consider that perhaps there is meaning, even if you cannot see what it is. Do you no longer believe in the sun when it is not shining? Grieving is a natural life process which takes time, as does any healing of a great wound. Take each day as it comes, step by step and you will go far.

III

About bereavement,
grief and healing

The grief experience

Aspects

Definition

Grief is the emotional state experienced during the process of mourning a loss. Pain-filled though it is, it is a natural rehabilitative process which, if unimpeded, follows a healing course through to restoration and regeneration.

A holistic view

My approach to bereavement is holistic because the whole person, not just his emotions, is affected; he responds physically, intellectually and spiritually. Not only the inner world but his perception of the external world alters too, for whilst mourning, circumstances are viewed differently and priorities change. Others may perceive him to be responding in unfamiliar and therefore disturbing ways, and so the waves made by the bereavement fan out with widespread effect. Grief is a pervasive experience.

There are times during the mourning period when the bereft person feels completely alone, like an island cut off from the mainland by an expanse of water. Yet deep beneath the sea the island is part of the land mass. So too are we all part of and inseparable from humanity, and thus it is that we can reach out to one another in compassion, and with empathy and understanding reach in to comfort and sustain.

Life choices

In dealing with grief, as with any other circumstances in life, there are *three main categories of choice:*

- to make creative use of the opportunity that loss provides;
- to struggle through to resignation and settle for that with a sense of victimization;
- to block the pain experience which, whilst seemingly an escape, in

reality interferes with the natural course of grief and only post-pones it at the cost of much valuable energy.

The choice made (whether consciously or subconsciously) depends upon many factors, the most central being *self-concept*. A person's sense of self-worth determines the quality of his living.

Someone with genuine self-respect and an easy affection for himself will not only feel entitled to growth and restoration, but able, in time, to achieve them.

The self-doubting individual, who tends to carry guilt because he does not feel he has the right to relinquish it, may choose resignation because he feels depressed, cheated by life, and not entitled to anything better. Long-term therapy can be most helpful to those with a poor self-concept.

The escapee is generally a person who is fearful of being over-whelmed by grief, anger or feelings of guilt. Given time, encourage-ment and a safe environment in which he can at his own pace risk facing his emotions, he may choose to work through the loss.

Views of bereavement

I find that there are *two* commonly held opinions about bereavement:

- that it is a lifelong victimization from which there is no real re-covery (often the attacker is thought to be an uncaring and some-what sadistic God)
- that grief should be dealt with and recovered from in a matter of weeks, perhaps a month or two.

Both these views are unrealistic and untrue. They account for much fearfulness and disillusionment in mourners, and for many of the most unhelpful and alienating comments that are made to them by people who do not understand.

I offer another perspective, without minimising the pain of loss, negating its significance nor underestimating the grief experienced by the survivor: bereavement can be a time of healing and of growing self-awareness; of opening to new perspectives and greater understanding if the mourner wishes to live his life in such a way that it becomes creative and a tribute both to the living and the deceased.

When our teenage daughter was seriously hurt in a motor-accident some years ago the consultant told us there was a mere 20% chance of her recovery. I realised then that if I could not in some way use that terrible experience to good effect, life would be without much meaning and I would become afraid of living.

If work with the bereaved offers the creative perspective of choice, it does more than give assistance during the period of grief: it facilitates an awareness of positive opportunities that are present both at that time and after recovery. Grieving then becomes life-affirming, and indeed there is more to life than just surviving.

Dynamics

The pattern of grief

The grief experience is coloured to a great extent by the circumstances of the death. Was it sudden and unexpected, long-awaited, violent . . .? The pattern of grief, whatever the cause of death, follows a somewhat definable course, the main variants being the personality, past experiences of the mourner, the potency of the emotions, and the duration of the grieving period.

The process of mourning begins with a diagnosis, with a relapse (when it becomes clear after a remission of illness that the person will die), or when death occurs or news thereof is received.

The first reaction is one of shock – that sense of being stunned – nature's tranquilliser. It may last for days or even weeks. As it begins to recede and the still unbelievable and seemingly unacceptable reality begins to sink in, the pain increases. This is a mark of progress, for grief cannot be worked through unless the fact of death is acknowledged. When it is, the pain intensifies.

The range of symptoms (which represent the protestation, anger, disbelief, and later the reactive depression of grief) are experienced with varied intensity. They interchange from moment to moment, hour to hour, or day to day. Their variation is wide and their potency can be frightening. Resistance to the painful and untenable truth can be strong. It may take the form of a refusal even to acknowledge the event of death (though this does not normally last long), denial, disbelief, or escape into the distraction of some activity such as work. All of these are attempts to avoid the flooding in of what is feared to be insupportable grief. With time the severity of the pain begins to lessen, though deep sorrow is still present; the "bad days" become not only less frequent but also less severe. This progress through the mourning period is greatly facilitated by the acceptance and appropriate expression of all the feelings that arise. Blocking them interferes with the grief process.

Time-frames cannot be set for the different phases of mourning, yet research indicates that at approximately six months after a loss, when the severity of grief has to some extent abated, it intensifies again for a limited period. It has been my experience that this increase occurs at about four to five months after the death. I believe that this indicates that grief counselling speeds up the process of working through the loss. Research is generally conducted with subjects who are not receiving any form of professional help.

This second upsurge of grief seems to come when the mourner is feeling calmer, able to laugh again (having initially believed that any form of pleasure in living had died with the loved one), and is beginning to gather up the threads of normal life. Suddenly he realises that this change is taking place and yet the one he so misses will not return. The irreversibility of the loss, his feelings of impotence, and disloyalty relating to his process of healing arise in an upheaval of anguish and confusion. All this must subside again before he can reach the calmer period of readjustment that is beyond.

Counselling can, in both the earlier and this period of mourning, be useful and meaningful.

The anniversary of the death is generally a time of great sadness and painful remembering, as are celebrations such as birthdays, Christmas, New Year, Passover, other significant holidays, vacations and times of family togetherness. For the person left on his own, the sense of bereftness is even more acute. Associations with these special days accentuate the loss, especially during the first year of bereavement.

No time limit can be set for grief which may continue for a year, eighteen months, two years and more. This depends upon the significance of the loss and other factors (discussed on p. 154). Perhaps one of the most important is choice. Throughout the mourning period the experience is a changing one. It is essential to encourage the griever in the early stages of grief that whilst a great loss takes a long time to work through, his pain will not remain so acute. His feelings will ebb, flow and change with periods of respite in between.

Mourning is complete when restoration of the loved one has taken place within the survivor through the establishment of a changed relationship with him/her. Energy is then freed for new investment in living. (See "Restoration", p. 52.)

Residues of feelings emerge from time to time triggered by associations. If grief has been adequately worked through these are isolated and infrequent stabs of sorrow which are of short duration.

The experience

Even the most common manifestations of grief vary from person to person. They can be categorized as follows:

● *Physical symptoms*
Loss of appetite or compensatory overeating with resultant weight loss or gain; difficulty in or need for repeated swallowing; heaviness or pain in the chest area or abdomen; digestive upsets; dryness of mouth; emptiness; sighing; lethargy; muscle weakness; insomnia or escape into sleep; extensive tiredness; disturbing dreams; restlessness; headaches; backache; general muscular pains; symptoms of the deceased's last illness; a taking on of his/her mannerisms. There may be increased or a new dependency on cigarettes, alcohol or drugs (prescribed or other), especially sleeping pills and tranquillizers.

Diarrhoea and vomiting may occur during periods of great anxiety whilst constipation usually accompanies depression.

● *Emotional experiences*
Stunned shock, numbness, emptiness; helplessness; acute sensitivity; searching for the deceased; the urge to cry out, scream; agitation; insecurity, anxiety, fearfulness; irritability, anger, hostility, rage; sadness, pining, yearning; crying, sobbing – sometimes unexpectedly and with difficulty in stopping, depression; pain, anguish, despair; irrationality, fear of going insane; a horror of or a repeated need to visit the cemetery; a roller-coaster experience of alternating calm and turmoil; loneliness, a sense of isolation, inner cold and withdrawal; increased spending for compensation and distraction; difficulty in rising each morning.

● *Intellectual reactions*
Confusion; disbelief; questioning; searching for reasons/meaning/related information; a sense of meaninglessness; a need to speak about the loved one and the events of the death; avoidance and/or difficulty therewith; expectations of his/her return; lack of motivation; difficulty in making decisions, concentrating or completing a task; guilt-laden thoughts and regrets; preoccupation with the loss; role-outrage at not having that child to parent; idealization of the deceased; perception of rationality whilst irrational; suicidal thoughts; haunting recall of disturbing aspects such as symptoms of the illness, a last argument or the death itself.

• Spiritual effects

Questioning God, the universe, life and death for meaning; belief that meaning can/cannot be found; withdrawal from, anger with, or a closeness to God; focus on scripture and religion; deepened spirituality or a negation thereof; a desire to know more about afterlife; a need for spiritual counselling and support; awareness of, or a desire for the experience of the loved one's presence.

• Social responses

A need to be with people; a desire for privacy and solitude; difficulty with talking or a need to talk about the loved one and the loss; a constant urge to be active and involved away from home or wanting to remain within the safety of home; the necessity to keep busy; lack of social motivation; a sense of incompetence with regard to job performance, of lowered creativity and effectiveness in relation to work, family, and social circle; the need for support from relations, friends and colleagues, and increased sensitivity to any perceived slight or avoidance of contact.

Many survivors feel the necessity of a support group such as The Compassionate Friends.

This is by no means an exhaustive list, but it does give some indication of the wide range of normal grief reactions. Some or many of these will be experienced at some time and be changeable and of varying intensity.

Grief should be adequately expressed and dealt with because it has a bearing upon the total health of the individual. Therefore I emphasize the holistic approach in helping people work through their loss. Unwisely managed grief experiences, with denial of reality and repression of feeling, are likely to contribute to the development of diseases.

Grieving is a typical rsponse to loss. It is not an illness; it does disable the mourner for a period of time, but rehabilitation takes place if not impeded.

It is reassuring for the bereaved to know that their sense of dislocation and unfamiliarity with themselves and their lives is normal and that it will change and pass. The death of a child has a profound effect upon the family members and others, but recovery is natural.

Factors which affect the grief process

Although there are common denominators in grief (such as a sense of loss, bereftness, etc.), each person's mourning is a very personal experience. It is important to be specific about relationships and not make general assumptions if we seek to understand and be of assistance. The factors which to a greater or lesser extent determine the style of grieving are as follows:

● *The temperament or personality of the bereaved*
The presence or absence of ego-maturity, a sense of self-worth, style of and coping ability, resilience; the outlook on life and the choices made, etc., are aspects that affect the grief experience and way of dealing therewith.

● *The mourner's relationship to the deceased*
How significant is the loss? Was the child/sib the favourite, the eldest, the only child, one daughter among sons, the "difficult" one . . .?

● *How profoundly the survivor's life is affected by the loss*
Was the deceased a central figure in the home or living at a distance? Has there been a long illness with daily involvement in the nursing . . .?

● *The intensity and nature of the interaction up until the time of death*
Was this a closely involved or a more casual relationship, a love/hate interaction, a scapegoat child? Any one of these is not necessarily easier to mourn than another. Where there is self-blame or deep regret grief tends to become more complicated.

● *The nature of the death*
Was it sudden and unexpected, awaited, prepared for or not, a suicide, murder, from AIDS, by drowning or other accident . . .? Each of these has specific dynamics. (See Part I under the heading "Grief related to cause of death".)

● *Whether or not the survivors were present at death*
If not, it is important to know how the news was conveyed to them.

- *The amount of anticipatory grief that has been worked through*

Sometimes when a death is expected, as in the case of a terminal illness, family members grieve in anticipation of the loss before it occurs. Whilst the mourning afterwards can be as painful as after an unprepared for death, it generally takes less time to be resolved.

- *Previous experiences of loss*

The nature of these experiences, their frequency, when they took place, how they were dealt with, and to what extent they have been resolved, are all relevant factors.

- *The survivor's age*

Death is viewed differently at the various stages of life. The significance of and the ability to cope with loss varies markedly from infancy through childhood, adolescence, young and then mature adulthood, middle and old age.

- *The state of health of the mourner*

For a time grieving is a debilitating experience and exhaustion is common. Eating and sleeping patterns are usually adversely affected, and if the mourner is in poor health the difficulties are compounded.

- *Societal pressures and demands*

These fall into two categories:

- ☐ the expectations of coping and quick recovery, and related to this, that boys and men do not cry
- ☐ the pressures exerted by both educational demands that standards be maintained, exams be written, etc., and by the requirement that a living be made and business conducted as usual. Little "space", time or energy is available for grief work.

- *Religious and/or spiritual beliefs and maturity*

Generally these afford much support and comfort, though God may be rejected in anger and despair which, in turn, may evoke fearfulness and a sense of guilt.

- *The availability of a support system and the use made thereof*

Encouragement of expression of feelings, empathic listening, and regaining perspective are of inestimable value and greatly facilitate the resolution of the grief process.

The needs, tasks and challenges of the bereaved

To have experienced a loss does not leave the survivor a helpless victim unless he chooses that style of being.

As in every other aspect of life there are responsibilities, such as:

● *To physiologically counterbalance the impact of grief*
Adequate rest, relaxation, wholesome food and exercise are essential to offset the physical effects of bereavement (See "Taking care of yourselves", p. 15).

● *To confront and accede to the reality of the death*
This is a pivotal point in the entire process of mourning – unless the fact is faced, the bereaved are unable to work through their grief. To accept that reality, death as a physical finality must be acknowledged. For those who believe that it is the end of man's total being, the loss can be even harder to deal with.

The death of a child can seem so threatening that for a time the survivors have to protect themselves usually through denial, disbelief, distraction, escape in activity or in sleep. If the reality is denied there is great expenditure of the mourner's energy to maintain the self-deception. This becomes exhausting and can lead to a reactive depression because pain and anger are not being dealt with. In appropriate healthy grieving the tasks of adjustment are undertaken because re-orientation is essential if life is to regain its meaning. Avoidance merely postpones. (See discussion on p. 169.)

● *To bring feelings and thoughts into the open*
Insight and perspective can be gained when all feelings and thoughts are acknowledged and appropriately expressed. Grief responses can be bewildering and intense. When suppressed they gather momentum and can generate fear. The relief of release through tears, talking, pillow-bashing, etc., is an indication of the mourner's real need. When these thoughts and emotions are understood to be normal, manageable, and sense is made of them by connecting source and symptom of grief, the survivor begins to cope with the desolation. He is reassured, encouraged and finds the strength to go on.

● *To make use of available resources*

To find and use support and reassurance, whether from within, from an appropriate lay person (someone who is empathic, a good listener, understands the grief process and has common sense), professional help (a counsellor, therapist, minister), or a group – the obvious example is The Compassionate Friends. In relying upon his inner resources the mourner finds a sense of competence returning and renewed faith in his own strength. For those who seek outside help the value lies in sharing, feeling less alone and overwhelmed, and in the reassurance that what he is experiencing is a normal process.

● *To complete that which remains unfinished*

Perhaps goodbyes have not been said, and certain issues have not been resolved. The "loose ends" which trouble the survivor are the unfinished business of the relationship. Generally it is difficult to find peace before these matters are brought to completion. It is never too late to give expression to what needs to be said. The image of the child is held in the mind and heart of the mourner, and when spoken to (in whatever manner) can bring resolution. Often it is known or sensed what the child would say in response, and this too can be incorporated.

● *To recall . . .*

It is most important in the mourning process to remember the good and the bad times. (If all that has been experienced is the pregnancy, to recall that.) Whatever has been shared, whoever the child was to his/her parents or family members, such memories bring healing.

Lindeman in his research into the Coconut Grove fire disaster (USA) found that survivors who recalled their dead healed fastest, whilst those who blocked their memories recovered most slowly, both physically and emotionally.

Initially remembering is painful, but in a while it becomes a bitter-sweet experience and finally a great comfort. That which is distressing because it relates to anger or regrets, needs to be worked through if mourning is to be completed. Unhappy thoughts can be counter-balanced with the joyous ones that were also a part of the relationship.

● *To find release from guilt and regrets through forgiveness*

See the article on guilt and self-blame on p. 45.

● *To regain and maintain some sense of inner integration*

Grieving can feel like a downward whirlpool of emotions, one in which the inner man seems to be drowning. The recognition that the be-reaved person is not lost, remains intact and will become able to hold steady, should be based on factors perceived in the mourner, and shared because it brings great relief.

● *To redefine the self*
Often the bereaved say they do not know themselves anymore, so al-tered are they by their loss experience. Being changed does not mean that they will not recover. The new self emerges in time with re-or-dered priorities, different values and perhaps deepened understanding and compassion. Many issues need rethinking for, seen from an al-tered viewpoint, they no longer have the same significance. Discover-ing the newness is both interesting and challenging and, if self-affir-mation is part of it, most rewarding.

● *To keep communication channels open within the family*
People grieve in individual ways, with their own style and timing. Family members can get out of step with one another, and much re-sentment, misunderstanding and hurt usually results. It is most im-portant to allow each person his way of grieving and, as far as possible, to encourage the expression of thoughts and feelings. Update one another on victories – on ground gained. Sharing can bring comfort and closeness, but there needs to be a loving measure of sensitivity to how much a given person can cope with another's pain at a particular time. Yet overprotectiveness in terms of non-communication or mis-representation isolates. (See "Communicating is essential" on p. 40.)

● *To assist children in the family with their grief*
It is difficult for most children to identify their feelings and to know what to do with them. They need the assistance of an understanding adult who can help them recognise their emotions, give the reassur-ance that they are appropriate and acceptable, and show them how best they can be expressed. In the early days of grief this is often too much for the parents to cope with. Some other family member or perhaps a trusted clergy-person, friend, teacher, or caregiver can step in and help. (Part II deals with bereaved siblings.)

● *To realign the disrupted family structure and form new relationships*
Both the structure and functioning of a family are altered by the death

of one of its members. A "closing of the ranks" (structure) needs to take place and a re-assignment of roles or tasks (functioning) is necessary to restore balance. For example, if the eldest child has died the second one now becomes the eldest (or only child), and implicit in these positions are certain responsibilities and expectations.

Another example relates to the emotional significance the deceased child may have had for the family members. The gap that is left must be filled, and the now unmet needs be dealt with if recovery is to be complete. Perhaps a new baby will be born to restore joy.

Sometimes a death brings about the establishement of changed relationships outside the family: e.g. a lonely bereaved sibling may in time develop stronger bonds with friends.

● *To grant permission to cease grieving*

There are many reasons why parents and sometimes siblings continue mourning.

The most common are:

☐ survivor guilt – "I should not be here to enjoy life whilst my child lies dead";

☐ role expectations of the self – "What sort of a parent/sib am I if I can laugh and want to go on living?";

☐ implicit or explicit messages from the past, from role-models (generally parents) which the mourner makes his own: e.g. "It is not right and proper that I recover; Mother never got over Dad's death. She still mourns him and it's ten years since he died."

All of these are emotional handcuffs which the griever, in accepting them, snaps shut. They contain elements of guilt and self-negation. A useful way of working with mourners who are reluctant to relinquish grief, is to ask them what their deceased would want for them – lifelong mourning or recovery? This brings new insight, for the bereaved will do almost anything they believe their deceased loved one would want. I have never met one who thinks the deceased would trap them in pain. Another valuable question concerns what the survivors would want had they died.

It must be explained that ceasing to grieve is not disloyal. As grief recedes, the closeness within their hearts of the one believed to have been lost, reassures the loving family that s/he in essence is with them always, never to be forgotten. In letting go the discovery is made that it was not necessary to hold on for so long. Emancipation from grief is liberating. (See "Extended grief" on p. 32.)

● *Openness to the recognition of a context of meaning*

When a death has occurred, particularly of a child, family members in their pain and perhaps bitterness often refuse to consider any view other than that it is a meaningless disaster that has befallen them. Suffering that appears to have no meaning is the hardest to bear. The search for some context that makes sense of the loss, however unacceptable it might seem, may yield positive results. Death retains its mystery but openness to new perspectives can bring peace. How does this awesome event affect the values, religious beliefs and philosophical outlook of the bereaved? Can there be a deepening of faith . . . a new outlook on life?

● *To recognise and allow the unfolding of a changed relationship with the deceased*

Basically, we relate to the living in terms of their physical presence or absence, their availability and the relevance to us of their daily lives. In death the physical presence is gone, the sense of loss is usually acutely focused upon, to an extent that bars any recognition of the possibility of new ways of relating. To those who know that death is not the end, that the spirit continues to live, restoration of a relationship is possible albeit in altered form. It is this understanding that needs to be developed by those open to it. It allows the bond between the physically living (incarnate) and non-physically alive (discarnate) family members to remain as a creative force in their lives. (See section on restoration, p. 52.)

● *To reaffirm the meaningfulness of life*

The grief experience is one of changing moods and shifting phases. In time life can be meaningful once more. Willingness to be thankful, which means focusing increasingly on the positive rather than the negative, redirects energy into creative channels. Because the mourning process can be transformative it challenges the bereaved. The choice made between existing and paying attention to death, or living life is crucial to the well-being of all concerned.

Maslow's basic human needs model applied to bereavement

A. The model

Abraham H Maslow (PhD), a phenomenologist and former professor of psychology at Brandeis University (USA), has arranged man's basic human needs in a conceptual form that clarifies their order of development. The model is a useful guide to the bereavement counsellor, for mourning will accentuate those needs.

Diagrammatically they follow a logical sequence from the base upwards, stage by stage. If, during the individual's development, requirements at any one of the levels were not adequately met, the death of a loved person will intensify that lack. Extra care must be taken to meet it in the new context if healing and growth are to take place.

In diagrammatic form Maslow's model is presented as a triangle:

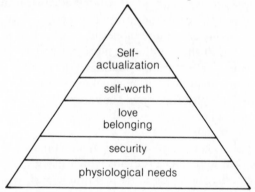

Starting from the physiological needs, we realise that all subsequent requirements are dependent on this first being adequately met. The infant will die if not fed, kept warm and dry. The person in physical pain is not free to respond to emotional support or spiritual guidance until his bodily distress is relieved.

Once this first necessity is taken care of, the need for security becomes relevant. It is essential to feel safe if the development of the individual is to progress normally. When we see the effects of insecurity at any age we know that the next need, to be loved and to belong, cannot be well-grounded: the person will not have developed a healthy sense of his right to be. Only when protected can he begin to realise that he is lovable and belongs to someone, a family, a group. This, in turn, is how man learns to love and find his identity as a worthwhile human being.

Self-worth is the next need of fundamental importance. Only when that is met can the individual move on to self-actualization. This means extending beyond the personal inner life to find self-expression in relation to something greater than and beyond the self, such as artistic creativity, spirituality, working for an ideal or a cause.

B. The application of the model to the mourning process. Clarification and challenges for the bereaved and their counsellors

● The bereaved person has, under the stress of loss and consequent anguish, increased *physiological needs* (for adequate nutrition and sleep) to counter-balance the negative effects of grief upon the body. The mourner usually either loses appetite, or over-eats in a sub-conscious attempt to fill the emotional emptiness within. He may have problems sleeping, or escape into prolonged sleep. Feeling physically weak and at times breathless, he stops taking restorative exercise. He may withdraw from physical contact and might turn to increased caffeine intake, alcohol or drugs (prescribed or not) for relief. These play havoc with his physiology.

Because libido is commonly affected by the loss experience, attention must be paid to further problems which relate to other levels in Maslow's hierarchy. Be aware of basic physiological requirements of the bereaved not only to maintain strength – and this includes the nervous system (vitamin B's) – but to offset the effects of an oft-present debilitating death-wish.

Strained and under-fed nerves threaten survival of the marriage. There is good reason why, in a hierarchy of needs, all others rest upon the physiological.

● Bereavement brings about a deep and pervasive sense of *insecurity*.

Suddenly there seems to be no protection from danger. The security of routine is disrupted and meaning seems to have been lost – a frightening sensation. God Himself is in question: there is nowhere to turn.

The lack of security may be so pervasive that it seeps into areas where it is not at all realistic and further undermines the bereaved: e.g. financial matters.

Assistance can be offered in many ways. (See "Bereavement counselling" on p. 165.)

● When a loved person dies the separation constitutes a break in the sense of *belonging*. The family experiences an immense gap in its structure, and its functioning is thrown off balance. The yearning for closeness to the deceased, for restoration, and the resistance to the reality of the loss, demonstrate how strong the *love need* is. There is a marked sense of separation. Much patience, support and encouragement are required to help the bereaved go through the experience of loss. When the marriage is shaken by the death of a child the sense of belonging is further outraged. Help is required with regard to good communication, understanding different styles and timing of grieving, patience and the willingness to compromise.

● *Self-worth* may have been intimately bound up with the deceased who perhaps affirmed the bereaved in an interaction that now no longer exists.

Self-blame often tortures the bereaved, undermining their self-respect. In addition, the feeling of being overwhelmed and unable to cope with the pain and anxiety of loss can play havoc with self-esteem (which is linked to personal competence, self-recognition thereof, and respect accorded by others).

Perspective on guilt, reassurance, encouragement, help to find an own way to resolution of grief, and contribute to restoring a personal sense of worth. In re-investing in life once more a new self-respect emerges: that of having won through.

● *Self-actualization* is only possible when the previous needs have been or are well on the way to being met. In the context of bereavement it implies having successfully worked through the loss, the sense of rehabilitation, victory and growth. Self-actualization is not possible if the mourner settles for resignation to (rather than acceptance of) the change in his life. It may or may not include a desire to assist others through their grief – a beautiful testimony to the return of competence and personal growth that has occurred. Deepened insight, compassion, and an ability to remain open to pain are all possible gains.

Bereavement counselling

What bereavement counsellors are dealing with

☐ Aspects of the grief itself
☐ The griever's own personal dynamics:
   ☐ his inner world
   ☐ his view of his outer world
   ☐ his past experience
   ☐ the present
   ☐ his future – goals, hopes and the loss thereof.
   ☐ the child in him, which manifests under stress.
☐ His social context: family, society, culture, religion and their effects upon him.
☐ Our own responses and reactions.

We are there to make it safe enough for the bereaved to risk dealing with his pain and to facilitate finding his chosen way through grief. We do not heal: we enable it to take place.

The information we should elicit in the first interview

☐ What was the mourner's relationship to the deceased? How close was that relationship, how significant is the loss, and in what way?
☐ How recent was the death?
☐ What was the cause?
☐ What grief work has already been done?
☐ What is the bereaved's general state of health. Is he eating, sleeping, taking exercise?
☐ Who are the family members? Are there surviving children?
☐ What is the feeling within the marriage?
☐ What support is available?
☐ Is religion an important factor?

165

☐ What does the bereaved consider to be his strengths?

☐ What previous losses, whether through death or some other cause, have been experienced?

☐ How has stress been handled in the past?

☐ What help does he feel he needs?

It is also wise to assess personal characteristics and gain some idea of context. Concurrent problems, opportunities for compensations, and other attachments are relevant but may have to be explored in subsequent sessions. If the death was very recent these factors will seem to the mourner to be both irrelevant and irreverent.

What counsellors should provide to assist the bereaved

● *Encouragement* for the expression of the various aspects of grief: the anguish, confusion, disbelief, anxiety, anger, despair, guilt and depression. We are required to provide a space for any or all of these to be discharged in safety: to accept them with steadiness. Moorings have been lost; we can offer stability and understanding in the face of it all. The safety provided can enable the mourner to manage without tranquillizers. Therapeutic distance needs to be from the problem, not the person.

● *Perspective* on the physiological issues of adequate relaxation, sleep, food and exercise.

● *Interest in the recall and review of memories* of the deceased child, the times spent together, of all that the relationship has meant. It must be shared and empathised with as an aid to healing. We are well-advised to personalise the grief for ourselves as counsellors by asking to see photographs and hear details . . .

● *Supportive listening:* It cannot be adequately provided by the mourner's social network. The need continues for months before release is adequate. Past unresolved losses are, by association, recalled during the current grief reaction and will have to be worked with as well.

● *Perspective in grief:* Mourners lose perspective and it is most necess-

166

ary that it be regained as soon as possible. Counsellors hold up a mirror to reflect the distortion of thinking and feeling that the shock of the death has brought about. Balance needs to be restored. We can find the positive to counter-balance the negative if we have an understanding of life's cycles, and faith. Great tact is required.

● *Reassurance* that progress is being made as mourning proceeds. This is encouraging, and is generally not perceived by the griever himself. He is too enveloped in pain and too subjective. This consolation helps him to believe that maybe he will survive this nightmare experience intact. The recurrent bad patches, the intensity of grief and fear of going mad must be acknowledged as normal and understandable. We may be asked how long grieving takes. It is so individual, but goes on for a long time if the relationship was deeply valued. What is important to say is that the experience is a changing one and the pain will not remain as it is now. Wounds do heal: one can live quite comfortably with scars.

● *Attention to guilt and self-accusation* (See p. 45.)

● The *"permission"* that mourners can be themselves and feel as they need to feel. There is usually uncertainty, so unfamiliar is the grief-terrain, as to whether what is felt is "alright". Insecurity is increased by well-meaning people who prescribe what they think is best for the bereaved to do. He knows for himself what he wants; what he needs is the freedom to follow his inner prompting.

● *Sensitive timing* is essential. Right timing aids healing; wrong timing might increase distress. Mistakes made with good intentions are generally forgiven. If we really listen we will know when to remain silent, what to say and how to say it. We should not encourage intellectualisations before feelings are adequately expressed and some relief is gained. Emotions take months and months of expression before they even begin to give way to some initial peace of mind. The rhythm of grief is uneven and so dependent upon outer as well as inner events.

Non-recall of issues that are initially too threatening to deal with must be allowed. We go always at the chosen pace of the bereaved. If he feels safe in the counselling situation he will eventually find the courage to open Pandora's box containing his fears.

● *Relaxation and imagery skills.* (See p. 26. Tapes are available from TCF.)

● *Assistance towards coping* with daily life and relationships during the first six months. Mourning is not a time for major decisions, but the competence to deal with basic practicalities, though difficult for the bereaved to re-establish, is encouraging to him. The section on marriage and loss will act as a guide when assisting with partner difficulties. Attention must be paid to that relationship. After the death of a child the marriage is under great strain.

● If it is of value to the mourner, an *exploration of the role that religion or a philosophy of life and death plays* in his grief.

It is not easy to silently share someone's pain, but often we have to do just that; sometimes there are no words that are appropriate. But the silence can be a quiet offer of support, love and strength. We understand little of energy flow, but it is happening all the time and it is possible to consciously direct it. We offer the healing energy. By living generously we set regenerative cycles in motion.

The grief counsellor's privilege is to comfort through alleviating the suffering caused by the loss. With the above skills, intelligent caring and empathy, we are able to do this. Having faith, we wordlessly convey it. We will gain through being aware that we are also, in a sense, working with the spirit of the deceased. S/he is always present, both within the mourner and as separate from him.

In my view, we have a great and loving responsibility to develop a creative outlook. Let us peel away the conceptual confines that pronounce conception to be the start and death the end of life. It is a great ongoing cycle. If we are clinging desperately to this one small though precious part of it we are unable to help the bereaved. The answer in living and therefore for rehabilitation from grief lies in letting go: for it is then that we find that nothing is lost: all is provided and complete.

The avoidance of grief

The avoidance of grief can result in any or more than one of the following: anxiety disorders, neuroses, depression and psychosomatic illness. In healthy mourning feelings are accepted and expressed, though it is no easy task.

Some mourners inhibit, suppress, or avoid grief for a number of reasons which, according to Raphael (1984:375-6) must be explored with extreme tact.

Reasons why mourners avoid grief

- Fear of emotional release, loss of control, disintegration, dependency on the deceased, and resultant fearfulness in the absence of his support or affirmation;
- sub-conscious obedience to parental dictates which conditioned the mourner as a child (e.g. "take responsibility for keeping the peace" or "be good and quiet or I will be upset/ill");
- extreme guilt in relation to the death whilst the perfectionist type of person will contain his pain, having to be the coper, available to support everyone else.

According to Raphael, in working with these issues it is important that there is:

- *Recognition* of extreme inner pain; difficulty in owning, tolerating and expressing it; and fears in relation to it.
- *Reassurance* from the counsellor that these difficulties are to be found in others too and are not beyond help.
- *Respect* for the defences the mourner finds it necessary to erect and sensitivity in the approach thereto.
- *Affirmation* and acceptance of the bereaved in his vulnerability, and recognition of how hard it is for him to let go of the deceased and not avoid the varied aspects of anguish.

It is obvious from the above that the fearfulness and consequent defensiveness of the mourner must be recognised. Reassurance must be offered that the counsellor will not proceed in any way or at a pace that will be threatening. The griever should be gently encouraged to take one step at a time as he gradually begins to feel safe enough to experience his pain. Indirect exploration of the fears, guilt and bereftness will have to be done so as not to provoke too much anxiety.

Repeated work will be needed in the areas of the past relationship (and details thereof), the death itself, and the family and support system of the bereaved. It is here that the reasons for having such difficulty grieving are to be found.

Restoration:
a counsellor's perspective

After the death of a loved one the relationship which the family had with the deceased, shifts focus. Because loss is so shocking an event, the bereaved are acutely aware of their grief. Their bereftness becomes their connection with their child and they experience it as complete. In essence true bonds cannot be broken and separation is only physical. But grieving is a natural response and it seems to the survivor at first impossible and later disloyal even briefly to forget, to laugh, or to feel part of life once more.

One of the tasks of the bereaved is to establish a new relationship with the deceased in terms of memories (one way of constituting immortality), and through recognition and affirmation of the living spirit that does not die. When grieving proceeds normally the sense of loss will eventually lessen and the mourner will experience a closeness or an awareness of the child. Restoration is taking place quite naturally.

Mourning is completed when the essence of the one who died is internalized by the survivor, who then realises that in truth the loved one cannot be taken from him.

But sometimes the bereaved remains involved with the loss and the deceased seems to recede. The grief is not resolved because the sense of deprivation blocks awareness of any nearness. The continuing experience is one of emptiness and desolation. This is frightening and interferes with the mourning process, prolonging it.

Intervention is then necessary to restore the griever to health. Memories must play their healing role so that internalisation can take place.

How to facilitate restoration

● Assist the bereaved to get in touch with the deceased by remembering him, talking about him, looking at photographs, going over his life in some detail. Focus on the child and the relationship with him during his lifetime. It is important to reconstitute this so that the parent/

171

sib once again experiences it. There is then somebody there to be internalised. Acknowledge the feelings towards the loved one prior to death. Explore and help him to validate those emotions by experiencing them as real.

● Acknowledge the bereaved's current feelings. If we work only with the past he may block the existing process of grief. The counsellor must know what the bereaved is dealing with and honour that, so that there is no negation of any aspect of his present experience.

● It may be very important to model the art of "hanging loose" – of coping with not having the answers. Often there seem to be no satisfactory replies to the questions which persist. Westerners try too hard to gain control by finding reasons, labelling. It might be useful to explore why answers are so important. What is he trying to establish and why? Maybe acceptance is being blocked by this need for logic and domination. Perhaps the hook that he feels he is on is not a hook at all. To some extent we constitute our own reality. Restoration may lie in becoming more open-minded and spacious so that release of matters that interfere can take place.

● Perhaps there is a need in the mourner for forgiveness of both himself and the deceased son/daughter/sibling. Anger can lock him into one position in the grief process and prevent appropriate restoration of the child who is acceptable.

● Even if the relationship was unhealthy, difficult, strained, an important distinction must be made between being (essence) and doing (actions). Someone can still be loved whilst what he is doing is unacceptable. The behaviour is not the person; he is restored when the relationship is freed by this realisation.

● Honouring reality is very important. If the deceased child is placed on a pedestal, perceived as having been perfect, mourning cannot be completed because only one side of the truth is being acknowledged. Restoration relates to reality and wholeness. Make it safe for the bereaved to recognise negative aspects of the loved one by honouring the totality of both the survivor and the deceased. There must be no criticism, or judgement. The only way for us to achieve this is to honour ourselves. This does not mean that we think growth and change are not necessary, but that the need for them is acceptable.

172

• If the grief is for a relationship that did not have very much vitality or substance, it is the emptiness of missed opportunities that causes the pain. The bereaved will find restoration through our empathy, affirmation and encouragement to explore past interactions and gain insight. With adequate support he may choose to make some changes that will enable him to emerge from his experience with a new relatedness to life.

IV
Rites

Viewing the body

In the impact stage of shock and denial, viewing the body generally promotes the mourning process. It is difficult to avoid the reality of the death when looking upon it. It is only when the bereaved begin to emerge from disbelief that grief work can begin. At this stage the mind may be acknowledging the facts, but emotionally there is a refusal to accept such a painful event. Viewing helps to deal with this negation. If religious belief does not prescribe against it, it generally brings consolation and calm. It is a time for farewells and may bring family members closer together.

Awareness, recollection and expression are all furthered by the rite of seeing the body.

• Awareness

We relate to one another through our physical bodies: "Seeing is believing" applies equally in death as in life. Mourners have great difficulty grieving when there is neither body nor ashes because the loss remains unreal.

If no viewing and no coffin is present at a memorial service, expressions of sympathy may be less natural because the sense of unreality interferes with acceptance of the death.

With a stillbirth or neo-natal loss time is needed to say "hello" before "goodbye" can be said. This should be at the hospital, but some parents are too shocked and fearful to see and hold their baby then. They need a chance to begin to experience and accept the reality of having had a child before they can grieve having lost him/her.

• Recollection

Parents need an acceptable image to remember. After disease has altered a child, viewing him/her in the coffin may remind them how s/he had looked before the changes took place. This is not to say that the face should be made to look as if alive or sleeping: needs would not then be met. Reality must not be confused with idealization. The point is not the disguising but the honouring of the truth. (Thus the terms "sleeping" and "slumber" should not be used unless in comparison: "It is as if . . .".)

Kubler-Ross says that if an acceptable image is not possible, disfigurement can be seen, providing the family is prepared first and given time to absorb the facts. Some will benefit, others not. The majority of mourners are glad later that they had not only the reality but also the appropriateness of the death brought home to them. When a body is viewed any fantasies (they can be worse than the truth) are dispelled. At the same time injuries or malformations (for example, in the case of hydrocephalic babies) that cause death make it an acceptable alternative. This is a comfort, for parents want the best for their child. Thus, though no-one should insist, it is wise to advise viewing if there is visible distortion or trauma. When the head or face is too badly damaged it could be covered and the child's hand be visible instead.

Parents may want to hold their deceased child. This should be possible. Privacy should be given and they be allowed to touch, hold, talk, and cry about their loss. In hospitals or mortuaries it is advisable that a tactful staff member keeps an eye on proceedings from time to time to intervene appropriately should the experience become overwhelming. Perhaps half an hour is long enough to spend with the body in those settings.

Another factor in favour of viewing is that if death was by accident and the parents were not present they may now want to share in some way in their child's last moments. Seeing what has happened, what injuries were sustained, might be helpful. They will have a fair idea of the extent of their own sensitivity and impressionability. Once again there is no rule: some parents strongly wish to avoid seeing the body, wanting to remember their son/daughter as s/he was. This is a form of denial of death, but they have the right to their defences. They need guidance perhaps, as to whether or not to view, but not to have opinions imposed upon them.

● Expression of grief

It is hard to avoid expression of grief whilst gazing at the deceased, and particularly if s/he is already in the coffin. After a death mourners often try to distract themselves and avoid both the pain and the release of emotion. This form of denial is necessary from time to time, but grief demands expression and withholding takes a great deal of energy.

Not only are feelings voiced whilst viewing, but the bereaved hear what others say about the deceased. For emotions to adjust to a non-repetitive event repetitive behaviour is needed. Thus the comments and condolences of a company of mourners are vital.

Research done at the University of Minnesota, USA, in the seventies, revealed that after no viewing and quick burial there were reports of the greatest hostility after the death, an increase in alcohol, tranquillizer and sedative consumption, more tension and anxiety and the lowest positive recall of the deceased. Men in particular had greater problems in adjusting to the death.

There is little doubt that, particularly in our death-denying western society, viewing has a facilitative part to play in the grieving process. (Viewing in relation to children and teenagers is dealt with in Part II.)

The funeral

The funeral forms a link between the sacred, the bereaved and the community. Its therapeutic value lies in that the funeral:

- [ ] is an appropriate, socially accepted way of disposing of the body;
- [ ] provides a rite of separation, an opportunity for farewells to be said;
- [ ] underlines the reality of the death. It dramatises it, acts it out. The loss is no longer abstract. The funeral calls for action and therefore promotes mourning;
- [ ] has a supportive group confirmation of the reality;
- [ ] provides a focus of attention and motivates the offering of support;
- [ ] brings to awareness the realisation of how much the bereaved have cared. A life has been lived and has importance for the family and others. Its ending is marked with remembrance, tributes and thankfulness. It is a social statement of life's value;
- [ ] provides an avenue of expression of authentic feelings. Grief can be shown: acting is not necessary and psychologically this is very important. Suppressed grief leads to emotional and physical problems;
- [ ] is an occasion for the support of a community of people who share the loss, to sustain the mourners. This is a source of great comfort, not only because caring is expressed, but also because the people present verify the deceased's worth.
- [ ] affirms certain values that remain – that the survivors are not alone, and meaningful life has continuity;
- [ ] provides those attending with an opportunity to deal with both present and prior grief;
- [ ] usually is a committal ceremony of the soul into God's care: a comfort to those who have faith. It is also an opportunity to praise God;

☐ enables the bereaved to begin grief work and reorganise their lives without the deceased.

● *Creative funerals*

These are services in which the usual form is exchanged for leave-taking expressed in personal, creative ways. There may be a guitar player, a reading of a choice of poetry or something particularly valued by the deceased . . . If grief can so be expressed, depression is far less likely. It is rehabilitative to allow individuality to have meaning during times of stress.

I include in this creative category any wishes of the family members to wash and dress the child's body themselves. There are many parents who wish to fulfil these last rites and in the interest of healthy grieving they should be permitted to do so.

● *Private funerals*

Sometimes bereaved parents decide they want a private funeral – no-one attending other than themselves and possibly a very few members of the immediate family.

This is often the first response to feeling overwhelmed, and wanting to minimise, to escape the full realisation of the trauma. This is short-term safety at the expense of long-term benefits.

I advise against having a private funeral for the following reasons:

☐ Denial of the death and continuation of a sense of unreality go unchecked because there is no group of people other than the family to validate the loss.
☐ Morbid isolation is destructive to health, with adverse emotional effects.
☐ There is a lack of group support and few mourners with whom to share grief.
☐ Parents forego having tribute paid to their child by the presence of others who have valued him/her and who wish to be of comfort.
☐ The social group is denied the opportunity to pay their last respects and uphold the bereaved.

If parents, for reasons other than financial duress, wish to cut funeral costs down by having a private burial, they might be doing themselves a disservice that cancels out any monetary gain. People spend on what is important to them. They would be wise to give consideration to the relationship with their child to ascertain if anger or displeasure of any kind is directing their decision. If so, they may feel very guilty later when they can no longer reverse it.

In my experience, when mourners have opted for a private funeral and have been guided by the suggestion that they include their social group they are, without exception, thankful afterwards to have had a group of people there with them.

● General comments

To the extent that the family wishes, children should be part of the decision-making about the form the last rites will take.

Sometimes the parents themselves have differing ideas. Because the father usually makes the arrangements to spare his wife pain, her thoughts may go unheard. For instance, after a stillbirth when she is still in hospital, her desires may be by-passed in an effort to protect her. Perhaps the father is protecting himself from too much painful discussion and from seeing his wife's (or children's) distress. Avoidance isolates; grief is best experienced and shared.

Parents may not know that if they would prefer it, the funeral director will come to them to discuss arrangements, instead of their having to go to the funeral home.

A family member may be wanting to put a favourite toy or possession in the coffin with the child – and may be afraid to suggest this. Expression of all thoughts and feelings should be encouraged and the minister and/or funeral director should be asked all the questions that come to mind. If mourners are so shocked that they cannot think what they might want, they could be given all the options written down and the time to consider them.

It is natural to feel somewhat fearful of the ordeal of a funeral, but parents will derive comfort from being able to make and find it meaningful.

Cremation

Orthodox Jews and Moslems do not cremate, whereas it is the custom of Hindus, Buddhists and Sikhs to do so. Generally speaking the Christian denominations accept burial or cremation.

- *The advantages of cremation*
  - [ ] Needs such as viewing and a service with the body present can be met.
  - [ ] There is a quick, clean reduction of the body to basic elements.
  - [ ] Because of the immediacy and totality of the change of substance from body to ashes there is an emotional and intellectual realisation that life on earth has ceased and the relationship as it was, has ended.
  - [ ] Symbolically, oneness with the universe can be experienced when the deceased's ashes are scattered. Because in burial the disintegration process is slow the symbolic effect is not so powerful.
  - [ ] A more personal choice can be made as to what the family wishes to do with the ashes. There is a variety of possibilities ranging from containment in an urn to scattering in some chosen place.
  - [ ] It is usually easier after a cremation to move away from the area where the death occurred (e.g. if emigrating) – either with an urn or from the place of disposal. A fixed place of interment such as a grave tends to bind the bereaved.
  - [ ] Cremation can be less costly than burial.

- *The disadvantages of cremation* (according to a study done by the University of Minnesota, USA)
  - [ ] Those people who chose cremation and quicker disposal of the remains, without viewing, had least positive recall of the deceased and greatest difficulty in adjusting to their loss; as compared with traditional viewing and funerals.

☐ Widowers tended to choose cremation for their wives whereas widows chose burial for their husbands. This was probably because cremation is generally considered to be emotionally easier to cope with. Men are not encouraged to cry or indulge in other healing forms of grieving so it is understandable that (particularly in the absence of support from their wives), they should choose the easiest mode of disposal.

☐ Women are widely recognised as better able to cope with pain than men. This emotional resilience could be a reason for the wives' choice of burial.

A caution for those who take home ashes and, undecided as to what to do with them and (perhaps as yet unready to do anything), put them in a cupboard – supposedly out of reach of young children. There is no such thing as a safe hiding place from prying eyes! It is probably best that parents tell their youngsters what is in the box and where it is being kept until a (group) decision as to what to do with the contents has been made. Any curiosity expressed should be satisfied according to parental discretion. Some allow their children to see the ashes whilst others suggest they wait until the time of placement.

For anyone wishing to have information about Jewish laws and views on cremation, the Imanu-Shalom congregation has produced an excellent leaflet entitled "Considering cremation". It is available on request from the United Progressive Jewish Congregation, PO Box 17100, Hillbrow, 2038. Tel: (011) 646-6160.

Book list

☐ = Books for Children.

Augsburger, D. 1985: *Caring enough to forgive* USA. Regal Books.
Dass, R. & Gorman, P. 1985: *How can I help?* SA. Hutchinson Group
Downey, A. 1987: *Dear Stephen* . . . UK. Arthur James
Drake, S. 1988: *Though you die* UK. Floris Books
Fabian, A. 1988: *The Daniel Diary* UK. Grafton Books
Gordon, A. & Klass, D. 1979: *They need to know* NJ. Prentice-Hall
Grollman, E. 1969: *Explaining death to children* USA. Beacon Press
☐ Grollman, E 1976: *Talking about death* USA. Beacon Press
Grollman, E. ed. 1981: *What helped me when my loved one died* USA.
  Beacon Press
Grollman, E. 1977: *Living when a loved one has died* USA. Beacon
  Press
Grollman, E. 1987: *Time remembered* USA. Beacon Press
Hey, V. et al (eds) 1989: *Hidden loss* Miscarriage and Ectopic Preg-
  nancy UK. The Women's Press Handbook Series
Jackson, E. 1979: *The many faces of grief* UK. SCM Press
Jolly, J. 1987: *Missed beginnings* UK. The Lisa Sainsbury Foundation
  Series.
Kubler-Ross, E. 1982: *Working it through* NY. Macmillan Publ. Co.
Kubler-Ross, E. 1987: *AIDS: The ultimate challenge* NY. Macmillan
  Publ. Co.
Latour, K. 1983: *For those who live* USA. LaTour: POB. 141182 Dal-
  las Tex. 75214
Leach, C. 1981: *Letter to a younger son* UK. Arrow Books
LeShan, L. 1974: *How to meditate* UK. Turnstone Press
☐ LeShan, E. 1976: *Learning to say goodbye* USA. Avon Books.
Levine, S. 1982: *Who dies?* USA. Anchor Books
☐ Levine, S. *1989. Healing into life and death* UK. Gateway Books.
Luben, J. 1986: *Cot deaths* UK. Thorson Publishing Group

Manning, D. 1984: *Don't take my grief away* USA. Harper & Row
□ Mellonie, B. & Ingpen, R. 1983: *Lifetimes* USA. Bantam Books
O'Connor, N. 1984: *Letting go with love* USA. La Mariposa Press
Schiff, H. 1979: *The bereaved parent* USA. Souvenir Press
Slabber, L. 1987: *My kind is dood* SA. Lux Verbi
Slabber, L. 1987: *On the death of my child* SA. Lux Verbi
Staudacher, C. 1987: *Beyond grief* USA. New Harbinger Publ.
Tatelbaum, J. 1980: *The courage to grieve* UK. Heinemann
Von Schilling, K. 1986: *Where are you?* (Anthroposophical) SA. Novalis Press
Whitaker, A. ed. 1984: *All in the end is harvest* UK. Darton, Longman & Todd

Bibliography

Benson, H. 1977: *The relaxation response* USA. Collins, 78.

Levine, S. 1982: *Who dies?* NY. Anchor Books, 88.

Raphael, B. 1984: *The anatomy of bereavement* GB. Hutchinson & Co. 375-6.

Sarnoff-Schiff, H. 1979: *The bereaved parent* UK. Souvenir Press, 58.

Selye, H. 1986: *The stress of life* NY. McGraw-Hill, 422.

Spence, C. 1986: *AIDS: Time to reclaim our power* UK. Lifestory.

Staudacher, C. 1987: *Beyond grief* USA. New Harbinger Publ.

Tatelbaum, J. 1981: *The courage to grieve* GB. Heinemann, 83.